JUST A FEW OF THE COMPANIES & AGENCIES USING OPTICAL SCANNING SYSTEMS...

3M Corporation
Advanced Micro Devices
Allstate Insurance
Amoco Corporation
Apple Computer
Blue Cross & Blue Shield
Brown & Root
Champion International
Coca-Cola Company
Ford
Frito-Lay
General Electric
General Foods
the good guys!
Goodyear Tire & Rubber
GTE
Hewlett-Packard
Intel Corporation
Kaiser Permanente
Kelly Services
Lawrence Livermore National Laboratories
Marriott Corporation

McDonnell Douglas
Merrill Lynch
MCI
Microsoft
Motorola
National Semiconductor
NIKE
Novell
Pacific Bell
Procter & Gamble
Rockwell International
Silicon Graphics
Southwest Airlines
Stanford University
State of Minnesota
Taco Bell
Tandem Computer
Unisys Corporation
University of California
UCLA
Wells Fargo Bank
The White House
Xerox

What Schools, Universities, Colleges and Graduates are saying about this book...

"I must say that I am impressed with the direction and information you provide for those who are looking for an expedient process for developing a results-oriented resumé. **Resumés for People Who Hate to Write Resumés** *is one of the best books on the market for job seekers in need of a fast and effective guide for writing a resumé that will achieve the desired results... a job interview.* *The information it contains is up-to-date and loaded with tips that few resumé writing books provide.* *This book definitely lives up to its title."* **Donna Davis, Career Counselor, California Polytechnic State University**

"I have taught resumé writing for many years and found the approach you take in your book to be very similar to the approach I use when teaching. *I especially liked the resumé format provided for recently graduating students and the use of "While Pursuing Education" instead of "Professional Highlights" to summarize their work experience."* **Inajane Nicklas, Career Development Instructor, Diablo Valley College**

"Your book and its clear, step-by-step approach is effective for job-seekers of all experience levels, but I find it particularly useful for many of our students whose native language is not English. *Your concrete examples of skills and job descriptions serve the dual purpose of helping to alleviate the fears of resumé writing as well as promoting the confidence and self-esteem so needed for a successful job search.* *For students who are unsure of their language capabilities, the intimidating task of resumé writing is made so much easier.* *Thank You!"* **Shirley Kawazoe, Planning and Placement Center, De Anza College**

"I found this book very easy to use and the resultant resumé significantly more effective than the resumé I used for on-campus interviews. *The format is unique and makes my resumé stand out from the others.* *I would highly recommend this book to anyone who has trouble choosing the right words.* **My phone is ringing for interviews since I used this book."** **Sherry Cardeno, Recent College Graduate**

"Your new book on resumés and cover letters is just what our class needed. *So many of the books on this subject are too detailed for the average person to create a resumé from.* *With the job market of today, a person needs to give the hiring manager the skills they have in concise terms to get them the interview.* *Your book has so many great examples to follow and I especially liked your method of "Cut and Paste" to create phrases for a resumé.* *Your book gave our students in this session a new outlook on creating resumés and I know it will be a favorite with the classes to come."* **Judy Jensen, Amador Valley Adult School, Pleasanton Unified School District**

What Job Recruiters and Employment Specialists say...

*"I was very impressed by the way you were able to simplify the process of writing a resumé. Your book is an extremely important tool for people who find themselves in the position of looking for employment after working for one company for several years and have no idea where to start to look for employment, and most do not have any idea how to construct a resumé. With your **easy step-by-step approach to resumé writing**, you have taken the fear out of putting down ideas which translate their work history."* **Business Development Specialist, Alameda County Training and Employment Board**

*"Resumés for People Who Hate to Write Resumés provides the resumé writer with **a step-by-step method that will get interviews.** As a recruiter in the contract and placement business, I found Wright's methodology and format right on target for today's hectic job market."* **Bruce Homer, "The Writer's Connection"**

"What is unique about this book is that the author provides an all-purpose format that, with simple adaptations, can meet most of the contingencies the job seeker will face. It is simple to use, self-reinforcing, practical, and obviates the need for the job seeker to worry about the 'writing' aspects of preparing a resumé." **David C. Wigglesworth, President of D.C.W. Research Associates International**

What Hiring Managers are saying...

"As one who constantly revised my resumé during the job searching process, a book such as yours would have saved me time and could have opened up more job opportunities during that stressful time." **Charles Crohare, Branch Manager-AVP, Bank of the West.**

*"**Your book shows people how to write a skill-oriented resumé that hiring managers can appreciate.** I can quickly scan one of your resumés and determine whether or not I've got the right candidate for the job. Many thanks for making my job easier."* **David W. Green, Vice President of Finance, R. W. Lynch Co. Inc.**

RESUMÉS FOR PEOPLE WHO HATE TO WRITE RESUMÉS

A fast, easy, step-by-step
method to write Resumés and
Cover Letters

(Third Edition)

by
Jack W. Wright

2773 Carmen Avenue
Livermore, CA 94550

The author would like to thank his friends for their encouragement and assistance in publishing this book. Thanks to Shirley Ruiz, Robert Midyett, David Green, Joe and Pat Danna, Elmer and Evelyn Ayers, John Wright, Chris and Jackie Wright, Dorothy Quillin, and Gary Wilson.

Printed in the United States of America

SHASTAR PRESS
2773 Carmen Avenue
Livermore, CA 94550

Cover Design by Robert Howard Graphic Design

Library of Congress Cataloging-in-Publication Data

Wright, Jack W.
    Resumes for people who hate to write resumes: a fast, easy, step-by-step method to write resumes and cover letters / Jack W. Wright. -- 3rd ed.
        p. cm.
        Includes index.
        Preassigned LCCN: 93-087743
        ISBN 0-944020-03-8

1. Resumes (Employment) 2. Job hunting. I. Title.

HF5383.W5 1993   650.14
                             QBI92-20118

The Preface

What's all this fuss I'm hearing about optically scanned resumés? Many of the Fortune 1000 companies use, or are considering, the latest optical character recognition technology and artificial intelligence to scan, store, track, and evaluate virtually every resumé they receive. A resumé might be rejected if it is not skill oriented and written to the standards required by these new systems. These systems are also being used to automate and track candidate correspondence, such as "no interest" letters, interview invitations, or offer letters. Some companies have replaced the written application and offer you a seat at a computer terminal, and are using computers in a limited way in the interview process.

Optically scanning resumés is relatively new to many of us and the technology and the way it's used are still going through many changes. It's happening faster than writers can turn out "how-to" books and there's a lot of resulting confusion. I'm sure a number of these books will be telling you to write two copies of your resumé; one for the computer and one for a real person. *The format in this book requires one resumé for humans and computers, and it's the same format I've always used.*

ACTION VERBS ARE OUT - SKILL WORDS ARE IN. I've been writing resumés that hiring managers love for over 12 years and have always used a "skill word" format. Other resumé writers disagreed and kept promoting their tired "action verbs" and flowery descriptions. While doing the research for this book, one of the many companies I visited was Resumix, a manufacturer of optical scanning systems. When they tested a few of my resumés, I was pleased to hear them say, "It likes your format." The only changes for my resumés to be 100% scannable for nearly all scanning systems was to reduce the use of boldface and eliminate underlines.

The other new technology making it's presence felt in the job search arena is the "Computerized National Resumé Database". These computerized databases are the "Super Information Highway's" of the future for employment and identifies matches between resumés and the open job requirements of employers throughout the nation.

This book concentrates on skill words, and makes these emerging technologies clear to the average job seeker. It provides the information necessary to join a national resumé database, has over 60 optically scannable sample resumés, and is highly recommended by Employment Professionals, Job Counselors, and Hiring Managers.

CONTENTS

OPTICALLY SCANNABLE RESUMÉS

I first heard about this new technology when a client came to me and said, "My resumé was returned because it wasn't scannable. What do I do?" Even the classified ads for some companies are starting to state, **"All resumés are electronically scanned, processed and distributed. A <u>letter-quality resumé</u> is required for this process."** I called the company that returned his resumé and was told that for resumés to be scannable they must have:

> **Skill words - no excess verbiage!**
> **no graphics!**
> **no boldface!**
> **no italics!**
> **no bullets!**
> **no underlines!**
> **no fancy fonts!**
> **light paper only!**

I got a copy of the letter they returned with my client's resumé. It said *"Our company has implemented an applicant tracking system that uses a document scanner to process resumés. With this process we are unable to scan fax copies and resumés with unusual formatting. Our document scanner was unable to read your resumé as received. We invite you to resubmit your resumé so that we may enter it into our applicant tracking system. During the scanning process a computer will "read" your resumé by converting the text on your resumé into an electronic file. This electronic file is searched to see if it contains words or phrases to indicate that you may possess the skills and abilities needed for our current job openings."*

I was upset at first and thought we didn't really need machines interfering with the employment process, but I soon changed my mind. Simple put, an "applicant tracking system" means that your resumé is kept on file in a computer instead of being forgotten in a dusty file cabinet (if it's kept at all). It also means the employment process will be more objective. Companies are also using these systems to track their own employees to fill positions within the company.

After some research, I found that there were many companies making these systems, and that there were many differences in these systems. First of all, **all resumés are scannable,** and bullets and boldface are not usually a problem. Most systems will flag errors when scanning a resumé and these are easily fixed if the company has an operator to correct them. If they choose not to have someone correct them, they will return your resumé as in the case above. These systems can also automatically send response letters after scanning a resumé.

All of the resumés I show in this book are scannable, and preferred by hiring managers as well. The font you use is very important. **Only use common fonts between 10 points to 14 points.**

Some of the recommended **typefaces** are Weissach, Helvetica, Futura, Optima, Times, New Century Schoolbook, Courier, Optima, Univers, and ITC Bookman. Never use script!

The quality of your copy is also very important! **Copies made from copies or faxes** will not usually be clean enough, and laser copies are preferred.

Underlines should be avoided as the lower case letters often come close to, or touch the line, as for example in the word pay.

There are many different items to choose from as you go through this book. **All you have to do,** is to select the key words, skill words and descriptions that best apply to you, and put them together as shown.

This method is fast, easy, and you might even have fun.

The book is separated into the different parts that make up a resumé, and a sample is shown as each part is put together. For the difficult, time-consuming parts of your resumé, the "Summary of Skills" and the "Professional Highlights," you have only to choose from the selections provided.

THE HEADING

The opposite page shows how your heading should look. Set your page layout for wide left and right margins, about 1-1/2 inches for each. If you have the capability, you can use the **bold** function for your name. The address and phone number should be in normal type, and everything in the heading should be centered as shown in the sample resumé.

Additional Tips

1. **Your name should always be at the top of the resumé, and always use a middle initial if you have one.**

2. **Never use any other persons name on your resumé as it may confuse an optical scanning system.**

3. **You can put a message phone number under your home phone number, but the home phone is usually the only one given.**

4. **Don't abbreviate the state or Street, Avenue, etc. - resumés are traditional, formal documents.**

5. **Avoid Parentheses and the dash when entering your phone number as they can cause an error for the optical scanning equipment.**

6. **Never put your work number on your resumé.**

JACK W. WRIGHT
2773 Carmen Avenue
Livermore, California 94550
Telephone: 510 443 4327

THE OBJECTIVE

The **"JOB TITLE" should stand alone in bold type, match the advertised position, and not be lost or hidden in the objective.** Notice the difference in these two examples:

(1)

Objective: Position in the food industry:
*Sales Representative *Marketing *Promotions

or

(2)

SALES REPRESENTATIVE / MARKETING
Available to discuss a challenging and responsible position
where my education and experience can be fully
utilized to our mutual benefit.

The second example is preferred because the job title and objective are separate.

Companies are flooded with unsolicited resumés for every position imaginable, so when your resumé is opened with another hundred or so, you must insure that whoever screens it can easily see that it's for the <u>advertised position</u>. **If they have to search for the JOB TITLE, the resumé might get trashed.** For Optical Scanning systems, it is necessary to put in a space before and after the / slash.

The "Available to discuss a challenging position..." is pretty standard stuff and optical scanning systems couldn't care less. I encourage you to change the wording if you're worried about originality, or applying for a job as a Creative Writer.

You have no way of knowing how a company screens resumés. In a small company the receptionist might be the first to screen it as she opens the morning mail. She could be under pressure or distracted as she glances quickly at <u>your</u> resumé. That's why your resumé must clearly identify the job you're applying for and should be word-for-word the same as the advertisement.

If the ad you're responding to calls for a **SALES REPRESENTATIVE** - that's what you write. If it calls for an **ACCOUNT REPRESENTATIVE** - that's what you write. If the title for your job varies from one company to another, you can leave the title blank on your original (but leave space for it), and, after you've made copies, you can type in any title you want.

JACK W. WRIGHT
2773 Carmen Avenue
Livermore, California 94550
Telephone: 510 443 4327
SALES REPRESENTATIVE

Available to discuss a challenging and responsible position
where my background and experience can be fully
utilized to our mutual benefit.

SUMMARY OF SKILLS

The new buzz-word for optical scanning systems is "Keywords." "Keywords" refer to any word the system is told to look for, and each keyword the system finds is called a "hit." The more hits, the higher your score - just like baseball. These keywords can be skills, years of experience, character traits, schools, hardware, software, or just about anything the employer finds important. I saw a lot of resumés when I was a hiring manager, and the first thing I wanted to know was if the person was qualified - **do they have the skills to do the job?**

Scanning systems also want to know if you're qualified, and skill words are still the most important information on a resumé. I read somewhere that the average hiring manager will glance at a resumé for only 6 to 8 seconds before deciding to keep it or trash it. That sounds about right from my own experience, and that might be all the time you have to get the manager's attention - scanning systems are not limited by time.

Before there was optical scanning, I used to advise my clients to list their skills without being to too precise. For example, just stating that you type, without the words per minute (W.P.M.) was enough. How good you are at these skills used to be determined in the interview, but the new scanning systems require specific detail or it won't register as a skill (hit) on many of these systems.

Select your skills from the "List of Skill Words" beginning on the next page. Place a check mark next to each skill you possess, then arrange these skill words on your resumé (in the order of their importance) as shown on the sample resumé on page 23. In the previous editions of this book I grouped these skills by occupations, but many people would look only at their occupation and miss the skills listed in other groups. These skill words are so important that I've arranged them alphabetically to make you check them all.

It's important that you try to "think like the hiring manager" as you choose these skill words. Ask yourself which of your skills will be wanted for the job - and list only skill words that are **required for the job, <u>and</u> are things you want to do.**

For example - if you're a brain surgeon who can drive a truck, and you don't like brain surgery - don't list it as a qualification. Some people don't mind handling the phones but they don't like telemarketing.

I have grouped these "skill words" alphabetically, and many of them were supplied by one of the manufacturers of optical scanning systems. Please look them all over; if you don't recognize a skill word you probably don't have it. At the end of the list are some character traits (also "keywords") you might want to include at the end of your "List of Skills."

16

LIST OF SKILL WORDS

- __ ABILITY
- __ Account Penetration
- __ Actuator Servo Arch
- __ Administration
- __ Advertising
- __ Airless Spray
- __ Aldus Pagemaker
- __ Analog Computer
- __ Appletalk
- __ Analytical Ability
- __ Asset Management
- __ Autocad II

- __ Balancing Statements
- __ Banking
- __ Background Investigations
- __ Billing
- __ Biohazard Control
- __ Biopharmaceutics
- __ Block Plans
- __ Bookkeeping
- __ Brick Laying

- __ Credit
- __ Customer Relations & Service
- __ Computers
- __ Computer Programming
- __ Corporate Liaison
- __ Creating Displays
- __ Cash Flow Management
- __ Computer Literate
- __ Consumer Products
- __ Collateral Management
- __ Commercial Loan Operations
- __ Cabinet Making
- __ Child Development
- __ Concrete Design
- __ Community Development
- __ Consumer Assistance
- __ Cross-cultural Training

- __ Academic Counseling
- __ Accounting
- __ Acute Care
- __ Adult Education
- __ Aerial Mapping
- __ Air Pollution Control
- __ Amiga
- __ Analog Equipment
- __ Appointments
- __ Assessing customer needs
- __ Asset Valuation
- __ Automated Materials Handling

- __ Bank reconciliation
- __ Bankruptcy
- __ Budget Preparation
- __ Building Permits
- __ Biomechanics Certification
- __ Biostatistics
- __ Blueprints
- __ Bpa Audits
- __ Brokers Call Rate

- __ Collections
- __ Computer Based Accounting Systems
- __ Contracts
- __ Customer Quotes
- __ Cold Calling
- __ Computerized Systems
- __ Credit Checks
- __ Cost Estimations
- __ Compensation
- __ City Planning
- __ Customer Conversion
- __ Carpentry
- __ Civil Construction
- __ Correspondence
- __ Compaq
- __ Contract Negotiation
- __ CADDS4X

___ CAD tool Pathing
___ Concept Design
___ Capacity Analysis
___ Computer Security
___ Computer Modeling
___ Calendaring
___ Commercial Leasing
___ C++
___ Clinical Supervision
___ Copy Editing
___ Custodial Accounts

___ Career Counseling
___ Complaint Review
___ CAPP
___ Ceramic Tile
___ CPR Processing
___ Concept Design
___ Change Control
___ Career Development
___ Computer Aided Testing
___ Creative Writing
___ Case Research Methods

___ Dictation
___ Digital Equipment
___ Displays
___ Data Modeling
___ Decontamination
___ Diagnostics
___ Dynamic Simulation
___ Displaywrite 5
___ Demographics
___ Demonstrations

___ Data Entry
___ Documentation
___ DOSS
___ Design Review
___ Detailing
___ Drain Systems
___ Dividend Reinvestment
___ Distribution
___ Databases
___ DOT License

___ Educational Administration
___ Environmental Compliance
___ Estate Planning

___ Engineering Standards
___ ESFAS
___ Electrochemistry

___ Filing
___ Familiar with Hand Tools
___ Equipment
___ Financial Modeling
___ Food Service Management
___ Field Applications
___ Flashtalk
___ Flow Charts

___ Financial Management
___ Familiar with all Standard Test
___ Forecasting Sales and Profit
___ FIFO
___ Field Service
___ Field Engineering
___ Flow Diagrams
___ Financing

___ General Ledger
___ General Office
___ Group Counseling
___ Global Equity

___ Generating Sales Reports
___ Groundwater Hydrology
___ Global Sourcing
___ Gsa Schedules

___ Hardware
___ HP9000
___ Healthcare
___ Hotel Administration

___ Human Factors
___ Harvard Graphics
___ Hospice

__ Interviewing Skills
__ IRS Amendments
__ IBM 3705
__ Installation
__ ISO
__ Investments

__ Job Costing
__ JET
__ Journalism

__ LAN
__ Leveling and Grading
__ Lisp

__ Merchandising
__ Material Handling
__ Management
__ Meeting Planning
__ Municipal Waste
__ Medical Records
__ Matching Colors
__ MMS
__ Microsoft C
__ Military Sales

__ Negotiations
__ NASDAQ
__ Need Analysis

__ Office Management
__ Outside Sales
__ Office Automation
__ Optical Logical Device
__ Operation Audits

__ Payroll
__ P & L Responsibility
__ Proposals
__ Project Management
__ Personnel Reviews
__ Promotionals
__ Purchasing
__ Preschool

__ Personnel Assistant
__ Programmable Controller

__ Issuing Parts
__ Interactive Video
__ IEEE
__ Inventory Turns
__ Investor Relations
__ International Marketing

__ Job Fairs
__ JIT

__ Logistics
__ Lasers ElecOptics
__ Large Scale Systems Technologies

__ Marketing
__ Maintaining Stock Levels
__ Machine Transcription
__ Mainframes
__ Materials Selection
__ Manufacturing
__ Multitasking
__ Matrix Method Analysis
__ Manuals

__ Novell Netware
__ No-Load Fund

__ Office Machines
__ Order Entry
__ Optical Computer
__ Offset Press
__ Organizational Development

__ People Handling Skills
__ Program and Plan Implementation
__ Program Management
__ Policies and Procedures
__ Pricing
__ Public Relations
__ Planning and Scheduling
__ Preliminary Stress Analysis

__ PagePerfect
__ Packaging

__ Personnel Assistant   __ PagePerfect
__ Programmable Controller   __ Packaging
__ Painting   __ Plumbing
__ Process Design   __ Production Control

__ Quality Control   __ Quality Assurance

__ Receptionist   __ Research and Development
__ Retail Sales   __ Record Keeping
__ RTC   __ Repossessions
__ Reports   __ Regulations
__ Radiation Protection   __ Real Estate Appraisal
__ Realty   __ Robotics
__ Ready Set Go

__ Shorthand   __ Soldering
__ Software   __ Staff Supervision and Training
__ Sales Presentations   __ Securing New Accounts
__ Shipping & Receiving   __ Sales Plans and Procedures
__ Scheduling Staff   __ Statistics
__ Site Plans   __ Skip Tracing
__ Schedule Calendar   __ Secretarial
__ Spreadsheet   __ Sun
__ Sales Training   __ System Level Troubleshooting
__ Stabilization   __ Sales Maximization
__ Software Protocol   __ Spray Equipment
__ Surplus Property   __ Special Education
__ Software Solutions   __ Strategic Planning

__ Typing   __ Troubleshooting
__ Touchup and Repair   __ Telemarketing
__ Technical Writing   __ Training Employees
__ TEFRA   __ Travel Arrangements
__ Technical Training   __ Total Quality Management
__ Tuck Point   __ Targeted Customers
__ Teaching

__ Vendor Data Review   __ Verdix Ada
__ Vydec

__ Warehouse Operations   __ Word Processing
__ Wave Soldering   __ Wire Wrap
__ Waste Systems   __ Wordperfect 6.0
__ Wordperfect for Windows   __ Wordstar
__ WAN   __ Wallboard
__ XyWrite   __ X-Ray Reports

KEYWORDS FOR PERSONAL TRAITS

The following are some of the words suggested by Resumix and the first two editions of my book. Check the ad your responding to and make sure you use all the skill words you can.

__ Ability to work under pressure
__ Ability to interface well with all levels of management and personnel
__ Pride in quality performance and achievement
__ Bilingual, Fluent in English and _____
__ Innovative in developing work flow systems

__ Ability to Delegate	__ Ability to Implement
__ Ability to Plan	__ Ability to Train
__ Accurate	__ Adaptable
__ Aggressive Work	__ Analytical skills
__ Assertive	__ Excellent Communication Skills
__ Competitive	__ Competent
__ Career Desire	__ Conceptual Ability
__ Creative	__ Customer Oriented
__ Detail Minded	__ Empowering Others
__ Ethnic	__ Flexible
__ Follow Instructions	__ Follow Through
__ High Energy	__ Industrious
__ Innovative	__ Leadership
__ Multitasking	__ Open Communication
__ Open Minded	__ Organizational Skills
__ Persuasive	__ Problem Solving
__ Public Speaking	__ Results Oriented
__ Risk Taking	__ Safety Conscious
__ Self Managing	__ Setting Priorities
__ Takes Initiative	__ Team Player
__ Goal Oriented	__ Tenacious
__ Willing to Travel	__ Reliable

Many of my clients can't think of a single skill until they read this list. Then it's usually a matter of deciding which skills not to use on their resumé. Use only the most meaningful skills and traits you have checked. If you're in a specialized occupation, you might have to come up with some skill words of your own. **Remember, we are interested only in listing solid, meaningful skills.**

PROFESSIONAL HIGHLIGHTS

This is where you list your job history. It's traditional to start with your present, or most recent position, and go backward. Most hiring managers are interested only in what you are doing now, or what you *were doing* at your last job - anything else is history. For this reason you should devote more time and space to the last, or present position, when writing a resumé. I use this method (most detail and space for the last position) for all resumés.

All of the responsibilities listed on this sample (opposite page) were taken from the list of Job Descriptions starting on page 25. Simply check the responsibilities for your job and arrange them in the order of their importance. For accuracy and originality you can delete or change words where desired.

The accomplishment is a good touch and can add a lot of punch to any resumé. It does not have to be something you received a letter or award for - just something you're proud of that saved the company money, or made things run smoother. Accomplishments are always stronger when they are tied to dollars, especially when they're related to sales volume or cost savings.

One of the tricks of the professional resumé writer is to take advantage of the different ways that dates can be shown. Sometimes the month and year is shown, and sometimes it's only from year to year. Look at the two columns below. The second column has the advantage of making it look like this person has worked for at least a year at each job. In fact, one of these jobs lasted only seven months. Please notice that you must use a space before and after a slash or it might cause an error when read by an optical scanner.

4 / 91 to Present	1991 to Present
3 / 90 to 4 / 91	1990 to 1991
8 / 89 to 3 / 90	1989 to 1990

Never lie or misrepresent anything on a resumé, but you don't want to show things that could be interpreted in a negative way if you can avoid it!

JACK W. WRIGHT
2773 Carmen Avenue
Livermore, California 94550
Telephone: 510 443 4327
SALES REPRESENTATIVE

Available to discuss a challenging and responsible position
where my education and experience can be fully
utilized to our mutual benefit.

Summary of Skills

.....formal education.....experienced in sales and marketing.....customer relations and service....securing new accounts by appointments and cold calling....creating displays....promotionals....sales presentations....pricing....reports....sales plans and procedures.....customer quotes......merchandising....staff supervision and training ....excellent communication skills...pride in quality performance and achievement ....ability to work well with all levels of management and personnel....reliable.... professional....

PROFESSIONAL HIGHLIGHTS

Acme Sales, Inc.   4 / 94 to Present
San Jose, California
Sales Representative
Position responsibilities include the following:
- Relating merchandise statistics to use of floor space to maximize sales and profit.
- Creating floor arrangements, displays, and working with clients in product selection.
- Insuring orders are filled in a timely manner and immediately notifying customers of any delays.
- Facilitating customer awareness through individual sales presentations and productive sales meetings.
- Conducting customer transactions in a friendly, courteous, and expedient manner.
- Making sales calls on current and potential customers and initiating product orders.

Accomplishments: Opened 5 new accounts and received Master Sales Award.

JOB DESCRIPTIONS

You can use the "List of Job Descriptions" the same way you used the "List of Skills," or use the Cut & Paste method used by technical writers. When something is used over and over (called "Boiler plate") they make copies, cut them in strips, play around with the arrangement, and paste them onto their rough draft when they're satisfied.

I've included dotted lines so you can cut sentences out, and play around with their arrangement before you glue or paste them to your first draft. This method is faster and eliminates the problem someone might have in reading your writing (if you plan on having it typed).

There are so many descriptions, you'll want to check the index on the next page. It's not possible to list every profession under it's own title, and it can't be done for some occupations. For example, even though I've included descriptions for a secretary, a secretary performs so many different duties it might be necessary to look under the descriptions for "General Office," "Word processing," etc. But the list should give you plenty of ideas.

In addition to technical duties, an engineer might be occasionally required to look around and find the best vendor for some needed parts. The first description under "Purchasing" states, **"Sourcing and vendor surveys to determine the lowest cost consistent with quality, reliability, and the ability to meet required schedules."**

This is fine for a purchasing agent, but would be a bit heavy for what the engineer actually did. So delete some words and tone it down to say, **"Performed vendor surveys to find the highest quality parts for the lowest cost."** You can use these descriptions best by deleting and changing words here and there. For now, just look all the descriptions over carefully, put a check by any that apply to you, and cut them out.

Avoid being too technical. Don't say that you were part of a team doing research on non-organic, histrionic widgets for the Nishfit Project and expect anyone to know what you were doing.

Once you've cut four or five descriptions from the list, arrange them on your rough draft resumé until you are pleased with their relevance and order of importance. The most important should always be at the top.

LIST OF JOB DESCRIPTIONS

Accounting/Bookkeeping

___ * Reconciling bank statements and accounts, and involvement with inventories in an auditing capacity.

___ * Performing pre-audit of accounts payable files for conformity with company policy.

___ * Analyzing and reconciling subsidiary ledgers in relation to general ledger.

___ * Preparing journal entries, accounts payable reconciliation, and monitoring closings.

___ * Batching and balancing of checks for bank deposit, and preparing documents to be processed by data entry group.

___ * Auditing and balancing bank listings against documents rejected for lack of information or discrepancies.

___ * Retail bookkeeping, managing and depositing cash, calculating account adjustments, and preparing refunds.

___ * Preparing and utilizing periodic financial reports, auditing monthly cost journal, and compiling daily financial information.

___ * Handling accounts payable and receivable, payroll, bank reconciliations, billings, collections, and preparing quarterly state and federal reports.

Automotive

Mechanic

____ * Repair and maintenance of chassis, brake systems, transmissions, clutches, and electrical and hydraulic systems.

____ * Major repairs, and tune-up of diesel/gasoline engines utilizing computerized test equipment.

____ * Performing DOT inspections in accordance with company policies and guidelines.

Painter

____ * Preparing automobiles for painting by block sanding, masking, and applying primer.

____ * Prepping, sanding, minor body work, detailing, mixing paints, matching colors, and spraying.

Customer Service

____ * Preparing warranty claims, and deficiency and installation reports.

____ * Processing shop work orders, preparing final customer and internal invoicing, reviewing for completeness, and scheduling work.

____ * Assuring prompt handling of service calls, and the prompt and accurate invoicing of service and bills.

Airlines

Customer Service

___ * All areas of passenger service: public relations, problem solving, ticketing and reservations, and extensive use of company's computer system.

Powerplant and Mainframe Maintenance

___ * Performing scheduled and unscheduled maintenance, and safety/performance modifications.

___ * Training personnel in scheduling, tracking, coordinating, researching and updating the mainframe.

___ * Troubleshooting, removal and replacement of all components in the fuel system. Familiar with the use of A/C manuals in reading schematics and researching difficulties.

___ * Supervision of personnel on Time Change Technical Orders, Hourly Time Change Items, and in scheduling maintenance.

Apartment Management & Maintenance

___ * Management of (number of units here) units - renting, collecting rents, banking, remodeling, screening tenants, and credit checks.

___ * Rent control inspections, supervision of contractors, eviction and court procedures.

___ * Painting, plumbing, electrical repairs, refrigeration, air-conditioning, cleaning, landscaping, and replacement of floors and coverings.

Banking/Financial

____ * Conducting customer transactions in a friendly, courteous, and expedient manner.

____ * Maintaining detailed logs and records, organizing files, and performing various branch operations.

____ * Accurate performance of all computerized operations necessary for customer transactions and maintaining accounts.

____ * Packaging consumer and mortgage loans, and reviewing and completing loan documents with customer.

Computers/Programming

____ * Configuration of printers, CRT terminals, modems, multiplexers, and other peripherals.

____ * Complete testing, de-bugging and modifying all on-line interactive application programs.

____ * Building and maintaining a data base and library system, system security, disk management and archiving.

____ * Data entry and computer programming in different environments and conditions.

____ * Computer programming on (name of computer) and for documentation of programs and data entry.

Construction

___ * Constructing single family and multi-family residential buildings.

___ * Working closely with architects, vendors, and city building department, and obtaining sewer and building permits.

___ * Preparing all schedules and budgets, processing through public agencies, supervision of construction contracts, and maintenance of costs records.

___ * Negotiating with governmental agencies in matters relating to engineering specifications and approvals.

___ * Design, layout, installation, and inspection of plumbing systems and tenant improvements in multi-story buildings, homes, and office buildings.

___ * Scheduling personnel and coordinating production schedule to complete projects in a timely and cost effective manner.

___ * Supervising crews in all phases of construction and interacting with subcontractors.

___ * Installing cabinets and counter tops, metal studs, drywall, finish trim, crowns, chair rails, dentil work, etc.

___ * Repairing and painting of metal and wooden cabinets and mixing stains and paints to match existing colors.

Contracts

___ * Extensive administration of contracts, solicitation of proposals, selection of subcontractors, plan implementation, and review and evaluation of plans.

Convenience Store

___ * Maintaining and complying with city, county, state and federal regulations.

___ * Training and supervising (of #) employees, establishing long and short term goals, hiring, firing, revising store procedures, bookkeeping, inventory control, buying, merchandising and retail sales.

Customer Service

___ * Maintaining good customer relations, calculating account adjustments, and preparing refunds.

___ * Conducting customer transactions in a friendly, courteous, and expedient manner.

___ * Accurate performance of all computerized operations necessary for customer transactions and maintaining accounts.

___ * Maintaining files of customer records from installations, including services rendered.

Data Entry/Word Processing

___ * Recording statistical data relating to (project), and entering rewrites, additions and deletions using CRT input.

___ * Determining additional handling as advised by the system and routing to appropriate processing units.

Data Entry/Word Processing (Continued...)

___ * Typing invoice entries, releasing back orders, and sorting and filing invoices.

___ * Logging in and handling computer generated output (bursting, decollating, trimming, stuffing, etc.), and insuring the secure and confidential handling of all sensitive material.

Electronics

Assembler

___ * Working with PC boards, loading parts, soldering & desoldering, touch-up and repair requiring knowledge of components, color codes and schematics.

Technician

___ * Working at system and component level in the trouble-shooting and repair of digital and analog systems.

___ * Using system documentation and manuals, interpreting schematics and logic diagrams, and writing failure reports.

___ * Electrical assembly, testing, and troubleshooting that requires a thorough knowledge of cables and connectors.

___ * Electronic and mechanical fabrication of complex, prototype electronic systems.

___ * Testing, troubleshooting and tuning electronic components, transmitters, and transceivers related to information relay systems.

___ * Analyzing job specs and installing and testing broadband, toll, radio, power, and alarm equipment.

___ * Analyzing circuit forecasts, coordinating equipment installations, and maintaining inventories.

___ * Performing initial set-up, power-up, daily monitoring and final powerdown tests of various electrical components.

Engineer

___ * Designing and burning-in board loaders, transfer systems, and surface mounting machines.

___ * Designing modifications to manufacturing equipment to allow robot to override existing control systems.

___ * Assigning appropriate sensors, solenoids and other input/output devices which allow robotic systems to manipulate environment.

___ * Solving test floor problems and making decisions regarding device anomalies.

___ * Generating burn-in schematics, supervising tests and technicians, and procuring outside testing services.

Firefighting

___ * Rescuing endangered persons and property, operating engine pumps and using related apparatus, extinguishing fires with water or chemicals, and administering emergency medical care.

Firefighting (Continued...)

___ * Maintaining fire station, engines, related grounds, facilities, equipment and supplies.

___ * Responding to all fires and medical aid calls on a 24-hour basis, maintaining apparatus and station, and completion of daily logs.

Food Service

___ * Insuring prompt delivery of food, resolving customer problems, closing out cash receipts, and handling paperwork.

___ * Taking orders from customers for items on menu, suggesting daily chef selections, training new hosts and hostesses.

___ * Scheduling employees, insuring customer satisfaction, closing out cash receipts, completing required paperwork, and supervising the preparation of the main dining room.

___ * Kitchen operations, ordering food and supplies, menu planning, and quality control.

___ * Working with the Food Director regarding menu research and specifications, and training restaurant personnel.

___ * Kitchen operations, hiring, training, cost and quality control in serving lunch, dinner, brunch and banquets.

___ * Menu development and product specifications for lunch and dinners, banquets, brunch and buffets. Complete control of kitchen operations and supervision of employees.

General Office

___ * Administering office functions including development of work flow systems, supervision, accounting, payroll, mediation, purchasing, budget preparation, and customer service.

___ * Scheduling, coordinating, and organizing daily and monthly budget projects, and maintaining financial record systems.

___ * Customer service, invoicing, inventory, accounts payable and receivable, and time sheets.

___ * Preparing and maintaining financial system information and all related data and coding functions.

Maintenance Mechanic/Engineer

___ * Operating steam generation plant, maintenance and repair of pumps, generators, compressors, steam boilers and engines, bearings, A/C units, valves, turbines, condensers and distillers.

___ * Reading meters and gauges and making adjustments on manual or over-ride controls to bring equipment to proper operating range.

___ * Maintenance and repair of hydraulics, pneumatics and water systems.

___ * Maintenance and repair of all building equipment; motors, switchgear, lighting circuits, control circuits, and magnetic contacts.

___ * Repair and overhaul of high vacuum pumps and systems including electrical wiring, and repairs on piping, valves, and system components.

___ * Maintenance and replacement of motors, rams, piping, conveyors, chains, electrical wiring and cables.

Maintenance Mechanic/Engineer (Continued...)

____ * Maintaining all operating equipment and product specifications, reducing equipment down time, and installing new equipment.

____ * Maintenance and operation of plant projects, and maintaining spare parts inventory and supplies.

Material Control/Handling

____ * UPS and freight bill paperwork, loading and unloading of trucks, forklift operation, and inventory control.

____ * Reviewing movement of stock at all points of distribution in stores and recommending appropriate disposition in cases of shortages or overstocks.

____ * Maintaining a minimum stock level while insuring stores and customers receive proper service.

____ * Monitoring inventory levels and stock status of assigned products to all stores.

____ * Maintaining part history files, inventory files, product status files, order information, and engineering changes.

____ * Working with managers and supervisors throughout the manufacturing facility regarding the procurement function.

Medical

The Medical Field is too broad to cover in one book, so I've shown a few samples just to give you some idea.

Assistant

___ * Preparing patients for examination according to protocol, and maintaining and documenting patient charts.

___ * Basic laboratory screenings and venipunctures, cleaning, and maintaining inventory.

___ * Providing referral information, pregnancy testing, and patient counseling.

Nursing

___ * Patient assessment, medication, P.O., I.M., & I.V., supervision of L.P.N.'s, and total patient care.

___ * Pulmonary patient care including S.V.N. treatments, drawing arterial blood gases, and pulmonary function testing.

___ * Administering EKG's, assisting with flexible sigmoidoscopy, and back office procedures.

___ * Instructing patients in diabetic care, skin and wound care, nutrition, exercise, and total patient care.

___ * Cardiac rehabilitation, monitoring telemetry, and preparing patients for various procedures.

Paramedic

___ * Routine interfacility transfers, emergency and non-emergency transportation of patients.

___ * Emergency pre-hospital stabilization of patients prior to transport.

___ * Inter-agency networking in providing pre-hospital care for patients.

Pharmacy Technician

___ * Organizing, replenishing, and maintaining a comprehensive product inventory.

___ * Knowledge of pharmaceutical terminology utilized to contact physicians for refill authorizations.

___ * Reconstituting and preparing IV admixtures and syringes, prepackaging various bulk medications, and admixing TPN's and filling prescriptions.

Purchasing/Materials

___ * Sourcing and vendor surveys to determine the lowest cost consistent with quality, reliability, and the ability to meet required schedules.

___ * Sourcing domestic and foreign markets as to vendor evaluation and performance.

___ * Negotiating, executing and administering all purchase orders.

___ * Monitoring material flow from receipt to final product shipment.

___ * Resolution of supply, quality and scheduling problems.

Purchasing/Materials

___ * Accuracy and turns ratio for raw materials and finished goods inventory.

___ * Directing of all materials procurement, inventory control, product evaluation, and management of staff.

___ * Working with management and supervisors throughout the manufacturing facility regarding the procurement function, and completed cost/value analysis for capital expenditures for cash flow purposes.

___ * Interaction with receiving, sales, accounting, production, and engineering departments to meet product flow requirements.

___ * Entering purchasing and vendor data on computer and ordering product for various departments.

Production Control

___ * Outlining work procedures, assigning duties, and monitoring work performance to maintain production costs at or below standard.

___ * Coordinating and monitoring the shifts material and product flow to assure production schedules are met.

___ * Training, qualifying, and advising production employees as required to obtain maximum efficiency and productivity from the employees and equipment.

___ * Assuring production workers comply with company policies, work practices, safety standards, and good manufacturing practices.

___ * Monitoring equipment condition and scheduling maintenance for required work.

Quality Control

___ * Assuring that processes are in control and within company specifications by monitoring production procedures.

___ * Maintaining all required reports, records, and control systems.

___ * Monitoring control systems to identify problem areas and making suggestions to correct deficiencies.

___ * Identifying and making recommendations to increase yields and decrease failures.

___ * Participating in the development of new products and processes

Real Estate Broker

___ * Knowledge and understanding of the mechanics of escrow and qualifying times.

___ * Thorough knowledge of loans, points, and interest rates and how they affect the buyer.

Sales and Marketing

___ * Relating merchandise statistics to use of floor space to maximize sales and profit.

___ * Creating floor arrangements, displays, and working with clients in product selection.

___ * Insuring orders are filled in a timely manner and immediately notifying customers of any delays.

___ * Facilitating customer awareness through individual sales presentations and productive sales meetings.

___ * Conducting customer transactions in a friendly, courteous, and expedient manner.

___ * Making sales calls on current and potential customers and initiating product orders.

___ * Implementing sales programs and policies to promote the sale of consumer products and services.

___ * Consulting with sales personnel to generate sales and discuss problems related to sales.

___ * Developing new and existing accounts in a highly competitive market and territory.

___ * Insuring customer satisfaction by investigating and resolving customer complaints relating to sales policy and pricing.

___ * Finding innovative methods of increasing sales revenues, motivating sales representatives, and assessing sales abilities of new-hire candidates.

___ * Securing new accounts by cold-calling, developing sales strategies for various accounts, entertaining clients, generating reports, and demographic studies.

___ * Effectively prioritizing and organizing work loads in a constantly changing environment to meet daily and weekly deadlines.

___ * Reviewing sales performance to plan, develop, conduct and evaluate training programs for sales personnel to improve performance.

___ * Analyzing market to determine new sources of sales and consulting with management to plan sales campaigns to develop new markets.

Secretarial

The duties for a secretary are too broad to cover in one book, so I've just shown a few samples to give you some ideas.

___ * Performing work with minimal direction and establishing priorities independently on a daily basis.

___ * Making all travel arrangements, preparing preliminary costs, and monitoring the appropriate accounts for approval.

___ * Answering phones, screening correspondence, and typing memos and documents.

Security

___ * Locating witnesses, taking written and recorded statements, photographing crime scenes, property and people.

___ * Conducting background investigations with regard to civil and criminal history, employment history, education, and character-related histories.

Security (Continued...)

___ * Law enforcement in rural and urban areas; investigating accidents, burglary, theft, malicious mischief, and minor fraud.

___ * Developing and maintaining security and safety programs while keeping positive relations with all employees.

___ * Inspection and auditing of facilities to assure compliance with security and safety policies.

___ * Field investigations, telephone interviews, background investigations and written reports.

___ * Photography of crime scenes, processing and printing of film, preparing court enlargements and exhibits.

___ * Classifying, searching and filing of all fingerprint cards, processing of evidence and crime scenes, fingerprint comparison, court testimony and presentation.

___ * Determining when security incidents are infractions and write infraction reports when necessary.

___ * Private investigations with an emphasis in criminal defense investigations.

Self-Employed

___ * Store management, retail sales, advertising and promotions, securing new accounts, inventory, scheduling and supervising staff, daily cash flow, payroll, and ledger.

___ * Day-to-day operations, supervision of employees, maintaining all business records, creative enterprising, sales, advertising, and customer service.

___ * Scheduling staff within budget to maximize high standards of customer service.

Stock Broker

___ * Making sound investment recommendations to existing and prospective clients.

___ * Managing portfolios on a daily basis through the analysis of market trends and economic data as it affects corporate America.

___ * Analyzing various company financial statements, contact with corporate officers, studying in-house and independent research reports, and employing standard methods of analysis.

___ * Selling stocks, bonds, tax shelters, mutual bonds, and insurance annuities, and making investment decisions on corporate pension and individual plans.

Teaching/Counseling

___ * Curriculum development, budgeting, teaching a variety of socially and physically handicapped students.

___ * Teaching various subjects, often in difficult situations where adequate planning by regular teacher was not possible.

___ * Planning of daily activities for latch-key children and day campers.

___ * Planning and implementing classroom curriculum, creating classroom materials, monitoring and recording students' progress, and conferring with parents.

___ * Working closely with adults and young people in analyzing their capabilities and determining how they can benefit from training and counseling.

___ * Teaching new employees and updating course materials as needed.

___ * Course design and development, data collection, job analysis, course instruction, and follow-up evaluation.

Technical Writing

___ * Performing necessary basic research and liaison with engineering groups to prepare outlines, schedules, and budgets.

___ * Analyzing engineering drawings and reports and conferring with engineering personnel to obtain necessary data for writing description, theory of operation, checkout, troubleshooting, and maintenance instructions for manuals.

___ * Assisting in the preparation of page and illustration estimates for manuals, proposals, and specifications.

___ * Preparing sketches for illustrating personnel of block diagrams, schematics, data flow, power distribution, and wiring diagrams.

___ * Coordinating with editing and reproduction personnel during editing and printing of final manuscript.

Transcription

Transportation

___ * Rate quotations, assuring accuracy, and the application of appropriate rates. Also reviewing rates to discontinue the use of unprofitable interlines.

Warehouse/Shipping & Receiving

___ * Controlling inventory, stocking, ordering from vendors, blanket orders, and inspection of materials.

___ * UPS and freight bill paperwork, loading and unloading of trucks, forklift operation, and inventory control.

___ * Reviewing movement of stock at all points of distribution in stores and recommending appropriate disposition in cases of shortages or overstocks.

___ * Reviewing sales trends and adjusting the stock levels to account for product expiration dates.

___ * Monitoring inventory levels and stock status of assigned products to all stores.

___ * Maintaining a minimum stock level while insuring stores and customers receive proper service.

___ * Verifying a wide variety of material against receiving documents, and reporting discrepancies and obvious damage.

___ * Storing, stacking, or palletizing material in accordance with approved storage methods.

___ * Providing assistance regarding material requirements and completing all necessary documentation.

"THE EASY STUFF"

Before I cover the easy stuff, I want to say a few words about the contents of your resumé. What you put on your resumé is entirely up to you. The "Resumé Police" won't come and arrest you, but you should never say anything that isn't true.

You should have only a few blank lines left on your one page resumé, and these lines can easily be filled with the "easy stuff." I call it the easy stuff because it requires very little thought and it's just a matter of writing it down. The easy stuff is your education, additional training, certificates, memberships, strengths, and a statement about references.

Education/Training

Many people have attended college but were not able to complete their education and get a degree. We used to show this on a resumé by stating it in vague terms:

Completed Classes in General Education,
De Anza Community College, Cupertino, CA
or
Presently Enrolled in General Education Course,
De Anza Community College, Cupertino, CA

Most optical scanning systems are not programmed to read this because it doesn't show a graduation date. The following shows you one method to get around some of these system:

AA Degree in Business, De Anza Community College. *
* Presently pursuing degree, Expect to Complete in 1998.

Be sure the asterisk is separated by a space so it doesn't cause an error when it's scanned. Everyone who has worked for a while can usually use this one:

Attended Numerous Company-Sponsored Seminars and
Training Courses in (_____) and _____)

Sales and Supervision could be just two of many words to fill in these blanks.

47

Certificates

Here's where you can list any certifications you may have that might be useful for the job you want. List them in the same way as your education:

Certificate in Welding

or

Certified in First Aid and Personal Safety

Memberships

Once again, list only memberships that are significant or relevant to the job. Professional memberships and trade organizations should be on your resumé because they are "searchable skills" when being scanned.

American Society of Training and Development

Additional

"Additional" is a good heading for anything you might want to put on your resume that doesn't seem to fit anywhere else.

Strengths

This is a good way to fill empty space and say a few words about what makes you a unique candidate. If you're at a loss in saying something nice about yourself, look at the sample strengths I've included on the next page and change some of the wording to come up with something original. These contain many searchable "skill words and traits." You can always take parts from any of these paragraphs and combine them in an original way. I've also included dotted lines if you want to cut & paste.

SAMPLE STRENGTHS

1. Career reflecting hard work, attention to detail, and the ability to meet exact specifications as well as cost, quality and time objectives.

2. Positive and enthusiastic, able to communicate with management at all levels and direct workers in a manner insuring maximum efficiency.

3. High motivational level, excellence of leadership technique, and professional attention to detail supplemented by the ability to influence and stimulate others.

4. Ability to create and present an excellent image of the company and its services to customers, and to coordinate and communicate well with clientele and management at all levels and efficiently meet objectives.

5. Expert organizer and energetic, aggressive communicator with a proven ability to accomplish the most detailed, sensitive activity while remaining within the prescribed policy.

6. Have been successful in performing assignments because of the following attributes: qualified by thorough, practical knowledge and considerable experience in developing new marketing techniques, initiating and formulating new marketing concepts, cognizance of competitor's product line and the ability to analyze customer needs and to sell specifically to those needs.

7. Capable of initial program development and handling liaison with governmental agencies, private sources, and community organizations.

8. Creative and energetic, capable of the sustained effort necessary to see a project through from conception to completion.

9.   **Hard working, capable of 100% effort reinforced with solid and successful experience in all-around maintenance and repair.**

10.   **Career reflecting total involvement, high motivation, persuasive interaction and communication with people, eagerness to work, and proven leadership qualities.**

11.   **Multiplicity of experience and skills including carpentry, wood work, metals, plumbing, mechanics, general maintenance and repair.**

As an example of mixing to come up with a new and original strength, try taking parts from numbers 3, 4 and 5, and put them together like this:

(3) High Motivational level, excellence of leadership technique and a professional attention to detail. (5) Expert organizer with a proven ability to (4) coordinate and communicate well with clientele and management at all levels.

"Mix and Match"

The following list is intended to help everyone who has trouble with words. Simply mix and match by choosing any letter (A through G) from the "self-descriptive phrases" that describes you _ then select a number (1 through 10) from the "abilities" and put them together as shown.

Self-description Phrases:

A.   A dedicated professional with initiative, drive and the desire to excel,

B.   Fast learner, enthusiastic and positive,

C.   Strong in customer relations,

D.   Innovative and flexible in developing new ideas of practical merit,

E.   Solid background of effective _____ (management...teaching...customer service...whatever!!!),

F.   Excellent administrative ability,

G.   Career reflecting hard work and attention to detail,

Abilities:

1. with the ability to exercise prudent judgment in decision making.

2. with the ability to mold diverse elements into new and exciting concepts.

3. with the ability to motivate students, stimulate authentic dialogue, and humanize learning relationships.

4. with the ability to give 100% and inspire subordinates and associates to the same level of performance.

5. with the ability to quickly establish a positive and productive rapport with customers.

6. with the ability to insure manpower utilization and high employee performance accuracy.

7. with the ability to anticipate individual needs.

8. with expertise in diagnosis, design, and implementation of individualized remedial and educational strategies.

9. with patience, care, and a genuine desire to help people.

10. with a positive attitude in the daily handling of assignments.

An example of mixing these to apply to a **Medical Assistant** might be (C) Strong in customer relations (5) with the ability to quickly establish a positive and productive rapport with customers.

Just change the word **"customer"** to **"patient"** and eliminate a few words as follows: **Strong in patient relations with the ability to quickly establish a positive and productive rapport with patients.** You could even add a "marked by" and a #9 to the end of this sentence - **marked by patience, care, and a genuine desire to help people.** The possible combinations from this "mix & match" method are endless, and substituting from the list of "self-descriptive words" on the next page makes possible even more variety!

SELF-DESCRIPTIVE WORDS

In the "Mix & Match" section you could change words so the phrases describe you better. This short list of keywords is intended to help you with these word changes:

Active

Adaptable

Aggressive

Alert

Ambitious

Analytical

Aspiring

Attentive

Cheerful

Conscientious

Consistent

Constructive

Creative

Dependable

Determined

Diligent

Diplomatic

Disciplined

Discrete

Economical

Efficient

Energetic

Enterprising

Enthusiastic

Forceful

Imaginative

Independent

Logical

Loyal

Mature

Methodical

Objective

Optimistic

Perceptive

Perserverance

Personable

Pleasant

Positive

Practical

Productive

Realistic

Reliable

Resourceful

Self-Reliant

Sense of Humor

Sincere

Sophisticated

Systematic

Tactful

Talented

REFERENCES

References are the last item on your resumé, and should be in the form of a brief statement saying that they are available upon request. References and personal data used to be included on a resume, but are no longer shown. See the next page for an example of a finished resumé, and the statement concerning your references.

JACK W. WRIGHT
2773 Carmen Avenue
Livermore, California 94550
Telephone: 510 443 4327

SALES REPRESENTATIVE

Available to discuss a challenging and responsible position
where my education and experience can be fully
utilized to our mutual benefit.

Summary of Skills

.....formal education.....experienced in sales and marketing......customer relations and service...securing new accounts by appointments and cold calling...promotionals....sales presentations.....creating displays.....pricing.....sales plans and procedures......customer quotes......staff supervision and training......excellent communication skills.....pride in quality performance and achievement......ability to work well with all levels of management and personnel....reliable....professional....

PROFESSIONAL HIGHLIGHTS

Acme Sales, Inc.   4 / 92 to Present
San Jose, California
Sales Respresentative

Position responsibilities include the following:

- Relating merchandise statistics to use of floor space to maximize sales and profit.
- Creating floor arrangements, displays, and working with clients in product selection.
- Insuring orders are filled in a timely manner and immediately notifying customers of any delays.
- Facilitating customer awareness through individual sales presentations and productive sales meetings.
- Conducting customer transactions in a friendly, courteous, and expedient manner.
- Making sales calls on current and potential customers and initiating product orders.

Ajax Sales   1991 -1992
Hayward, California
Salesman
Duties included merchandising, retail sales, customer service, inventory control, and training new employees in company sales procedures.

EDUCATION

AA Degree in General Education,
Las Positas Community College, Livermore, California

STRENGTHS

Ability to create and present an excellent image of the company and its services to customers, and to coordinate and communicate well with clientele and management at all levels and efficiently meet objectives.

REFERENCES EXCELLENT AND AVAILABLE UPON REQUEST

THE RECENT HIGH SCHOOL GRADUATE

Your first resumé is the hardest you'll ever have to write because very few high school graduates have enough work experience to fill a page. It would be ideal if you could study this book as a freshman so you'd have the time and information to plan ahead.

It's important that your classes, and summer and part-time jobs give you experience to put on your resumé.

Some obvious examples for classes to enroll in would be:

a. Wood Shop to be a Construction Worker.
b. Auto Repair to be a Mechanic.
c. Metal Shop to be a Machinist.
d. Mechanical Drawing to be a Draftsman.

Don't take just <u>any</u> summer or part-time job after school. Make every effort to be selective and get something that gives you useful experience for your future job. More obvious examples would be to work:

a. in a service station to be a mechanic.
b. in a grocery store for customer relations.
c. as a sales clerk to be in sales or marketing.

Even a paper route gives you experience in working with people, sales, and cash flow management.

Another way of getting good experience to put on your resumé is by joining some of the many clubs and organizations your school sponsors. Just be sure they're related to your job objective.

The most important part of your resumé is your recent high school education. List all of the courses that apply to the job under the EDUCATION part of your resumé. Instead of using the title "While Pursuing Education," you'll be using "Work Experience" as shown on the example on the next page.

The sample also shows that with a little planning for the future, a recent high school graduate *can* write an *excellent* resumé.

JACK W. WRIGHT

2773 Carmen Avenue
Livermore, California 94550
Telephone: 510 443 4327

AUTOMOTIVE MECHANIC

Available to discuss a challenging and responsible entry
level position where my education and experience
can be fully utilized to our mutual benefit.

Summary of Skills

.....formal training in automotive repair......experienced in troubleshooting and repair......fuel systems......brake systems......manual and automatic transmissions ....cooling systems....customer relations and service....cash management....ability to work well with all levels of management and personnel......excellent communication skills......pride in quality and performance......competent....... reliable....

EDUCATION

Graduated from Amador Valley High School, 1994
Classes Included:
General Education and Computer Science
Auto Shop - rebuilding engines and performance work.
Projects Include:
Member of a team selected to restore and rebuild and antique car. Car won "Best of Show" at fair.

Work Experience

Main Street Exxon   Summers 92 - 94
Pleasanton, California
Assistant Mechanic
Responsibilities included customer relations and service, and the sales of gas and oil.
Duties included:
  - ♦ Maintenance and repair of brake systems, wheel balancing, and repairing flats.
  - ♦ Tune-ups and minor engine repair.
  - ♦ Opening and closing the station in the manager's absence.

Grand Auto   1991 to Present
Livermore, California
Parts Clerk
Assisted in converting manual inventory system to computer.

STRENGTHS

Fast learner, enthusiastic and positive, with the ability to meet exact specifications as well as cost, safety, quality and time objectives.

REFERENCES EXCELLENT AND AVAILABLE UPON REQUEST

THE RECENT COLLEGE GRADUATE

The format of this resumé is different because you need to show your education before showing your employment history. This is because your recent training is generally more valuable to an employer than your job history.

If you worked to support yourself while pursuing your education, the heading for your employment history should read:

While Pursuing Education

instead of

PROFESSIONAL HIGHLIGHTS

It speaks highly for a person if their resumé shows they have the drive and wanted an education enough to work their way through school.

The School's Course Description is useful to prepare the Educational Background (see the sample resumé). This sample is for a recent college graduate, but the idea is the same for the graduate of any school or training.

This format is much more powerful than the traditional format recommended by many colleges. A recent graduate with a marketing degree had been sending out her resumé for six months and received only 2 calls. After rewriting her resumé with this format, she got three calls the first week, and is now happily employed.

See pages 91, 106, 107, and 109 for more samples

JACK W. WRIGHT
2773 Carmen Avenue
Livermore, California 94550
Telephone: 510 443 4327

SALES REPRESENTATIVE

Available to discuss a challenging and responsible position
where my education and experience can be fully
utilized to our mutual benefit.

Summary of Skills

....formal education...experienced in sales and marketing...customer relations and service....securing new accounts by appointments and cold calling...creating displays....promotionals....sales presentations....pricing....reports....sales plans and procedures......customer quotes.......staff supervision and training......excellent communication skills....pride in quality performance and achievement....ability to work well with all levels of management and personnel...reliable....professional...

EDUCATION

BS Degree in Business Administration / Marketing
San Francisco State University, San Francisco, California, 1994.

Coursework Included:
Marketing Research, Public Relations, and Sales Management.
Advertising Theory and Practice.
Marketing Management and Salesmanship.

Projects Include:
Public Relations - Wrote Press Kit for the Kinetic Institute.
Creative Director for the San Francisco Racquet Club Advertising Campaign.

While Pursuing Education

Raymond's Men's Wear   1990 - 1994
San Ramon, California
Sales Clerk
Responsible for working with client's in product selection, and creating floor arrangements and displays.

MEMBERSHIPS

San Francisco State University Marketing Club
San Francisco State University Advertising Club

REFERENCES EXCELLENT AND AVAILABLE UPON REQUEST

THE MILITARY RESUMÉ

Be sure to read the rest of this book because the format and other information is important to you as well as civilians. The resumé on the next page is shown to provide a general idea of some of the skills <u>we all</u> learned while serving our country. The only difficulty is when there's no civilian equivalent of your job (specialty) in the military. For example, there's not much call for ordinance handlers and weapons experts, so we have to concentrate on the other skills you learned. This sample resumé is made up entirely of collateral duty skills.

Complete the "Summary of Skills" that starts on page 16 of this book. Be sure to list the skills you learned from your military schools and training before the general skills that I picked. I just used these as an example, and you will be replacing the least important of these skills with skills of your own.

You will need to go through all of the "Job Descriptions," beginning on page 24, to find those that apply to you. I've gone through these descriptions for the sample resumé, changed a few words, and came up with some descriptions that apply to nearly everyone in the service. This is possible because we've all had the duty, stood a watch, and were trained in fire fighting, safety procedures, etc. All noncoms and petty officers have had some supervisory experience, and collateral duties in Quality Control, Training, Supervision, Security, and Documentation, etc..

The sample resumé is weak because it's not focused, and that's because I'm trying to show general skills. It will become much stronger when you use descriptive skills from your own special training and experience.

Education should include all schools, both military and civilian, that would help you get the job you want. Copies of commendations, letters, and awards should be taken with you to the interview, and never sent with your resumé.

In addition to joining the Defense Outplacement Referral System (DORS) and the Transition Bulletin Board (TBB), I highly recommend joining a civilian national resumé database such as SkillSearch (see page 130).

Be sure to read my "Tips for the Interview." One of the most common mistakes when leaving the military is to start working for less money than you're worth!

Samples of the military resumé on pages 75 & 81

JACK W. WRIGHT
2773 Carmen Avenue
Livermore, California 94550
Telephone: 510 443 4327
(JOB TITLE)
Available to discuss a challenging and responsible position
where my education and experience can be fully
utilized to our mutual benefit.

Summary of Skills

....formal training.....experienced in staff supervision and training......reports...... documentation......record keeping......inventory control......quality control...... planning and scheduling.....safety and security procedures.....creative problem solver......career desire......excellent communication skills......ability to work well with all levels of management and personnel....pride in quality performance and achievement.....reliable....professional....

PROFESSIONAL HIGHLIGHTS

US Navy   1990 to Present
NAS Alameda, California
(Rating / Rank)
Worked in the (Supply Depot, Avionics Shop, etc.) as a (Supply Clerk, Technician, etc.). Responsibilities included:
- Training new personnel and updating training documentation and records as required.
- Inspection and auditing of facilities to assure work loads in a constantly changing environment to meet daily and weekly schedules.
- Resolution of supply, safety, and manpower problems.
- Recording statistical data relating to work, and entering rewrites, additions, and deletions.
- Performing scheduled and unscheduled maintenance, and safety modifications.

EDUCATION
Graduated from US Navy (Subject) Class "A" School,
Millington, Tennessee, 1989.
(All training related to new career)

STRENGTHS

Career reflecting professional attention to detail, safety, hard work, and the ability to meet exact specifications as well as cost, quality and time objectives.

REFERENCES EXCELLENT AND AVAILABLE UPON REQUEST

MIDDLE-MANAGEMENT RESUMÉS

Sometimes a one-page resumé does not provide enough space to show your experience and accomplishments. The following sample is an effective way to combine a resumé and cover letter. This method lists your "skill words" in the cover letter, and has the advantage of providing more space while appearing to be a one-page resumé. You still need to read the rest of the book, and use the "Summary of Skills" section to assemble your list of skills.

It's important with this format that the cover letter and resumé stay together (using a special resumé paper will help), and you'll notice that the heading, with the name, address, and phone number, are on both the cover letter and the resumé. This concept gives you the option of being able to use a presentation folder with your resumé. The folder costs more, so many of my clients prefer to send it to the companies they really want to impress, and to the other companies they send it without the folder, as a cover letter and resumé -- a very cost-effective option. Desktop Impressions makes a full line of presentation folders and matching resumé paper, and you can call their toll-free number, (800) 545-4628, to find the nearest retailer or order direct. It will make your resumé stand out from the competition and is well worth the extra effort.

Although the presentation folder is more expensive, it nearly guarantees that the hiring manager will see your resumé because it's just too attractive and prestigious to be trashed. It's not just for middle-managers, and anyone in sales, or making more than $35,000 annually, can feel confident about using this format (with or without the presentation folder). Some people use the presentation folder for the resumé they take along for the interview, and mail the resumé without the presentation folder to companies that use optical scanning systems.

I've shown the middle-management sample resumé on the next three pages to try to give you an idea of what it will look like in the presentation folder. The outside of the folders I like are charcoal or ivory colored, with the words "RESUMÉ" and "CONFIDENTIAL" in silver for the charcoal and gold for the ivory. The folder is made from a heavy paper stock and opens like a menu to show your resumé.

Do not use the presentation folder for your resumé if you're not comfortable with it. One of the most important things I want to accomplish when I write a client's resumé is to make them feel good about themselves. This "feeling good" promotes confidence, and that confidence will come across in the interview.

Resumé

CONFIDENTIAL

JACK W. WRIGHT

2773 Carmen Avenue
Livermore, California 94554
Telephone: 510 443 4327

Please accept this letter and my resumé as an expressed interest in the position of Division Manager where my experience can be immediately and profitably utilized to our mutual benefit.

As you can see by my resumé, my experience has provided me with proficiency in the following key areas:

....managing food services, mail services, travel services, special disbursements and conferences... policy & procedures, contract 48 requirements and applicable DOE, federal, and state regulations....sourced and negotiated contracts for travel and food services....managing human & financial resources for several diverse divisions....skilled in implementing cost effective systems and business practices....developing policies & procedures for local government...extensive interaction with DOE senior management, and local government officials....

I am confident I could provide many valuable contributions to your organization's work, and shall welcome the opportunity to discuss this with you further. If I can provide any additional information, please contact me at my home address or telephone at your earliest convenience.

Thank you for your time and courtesy in reviewing this material and for your forthcoming response.

Sincerely,

Jack W. Wright

JACK W. WRIGHT
2773 Carmen Avenue
Livermore, California 94550
Telephone: 510 443 4327

PROFESSIONAL HIGHLIGHTS

Triad Corporation   7/ 87 to Present
Livermore, California
Division Leader Business Support
Responsibilities include management of property, supplemental labor, food services, business machines, disbursements, records, conferences and intra-university transactions.
Accomplishments: Developed policy and procedures for food services, special disbursements, petty cash, memberships, food donations, and intra-campus funding agreements. Performed study that resulted in elimination of leased and rented copiers for a cost savings of 1.2 million a year.

City of Pleasanton   7/ 78 - 7/ 87
Pleasanton, California
Director of Purchasing / Systems Manager
Responsibilities included the managing of purchasing, systems development, reproduction, mailing, stores, delivery, inventory control, and cafeteria programs.
Accomplishments: Designed automated and integrated purchasing, receiving, and inventory control system. Managed citywide training on purchasing and contract administration. Wrote and published the cities first purchasing and stores manual.

EDUCATION
MS Degree in Management of Science Systems, University of Southern California
BS Degree in Business Administration, UC Berkeley.

CERTIFICATIONS
Certified Purchasing Manager - National Association of Purchasing Management
Certified Systems Professional - Association of Systems Managers

STRENGTHS
Expert organizer and energetic, aggressive communicator with a proven ability to accomplish the most detailed, sensitive activity while remaining within the prescribed policy.

REFERENCES EXCELLENT AND AVAILABLE UPON REQUEST

HOW TO WRITE A GENERAL PURPOSE COVER LETTER

If you've never written a cover letter before, and don't want to write one because you have nothing to say, then just copy the sample cover letter on the next page.

Everyone has their own opinion about cover letters, so why should I be any different? I have always felt that matters like relocating, or sale of real estate, etc. should be discussed during the interview, and that any special skills should be on the resumé.

On the other hand, cover letters can help in setting the stage for your resumé, and if it's well written, it can reflect your communication skills and professionalism. They may not even be seen by the hiring manager, but can be most helpful in getting your resumé through the screening process. The cover letter should demonstrate that you're professional and courteous without seeming to "suck up." It's also a good place to mention any special circumstances, such as being unemployed for a long period. This kind of cover letter is shown on page 66, and my standard cover letter is shown on the next page.

If you have the name of the person who's going to receive your letter, be sure to use it - see the sample below. Many ads instruct you to send your resumé to the Personnel Department or to a PO box.

> Mr. John Smith, Personnel Mgr.
> Shastar Press
> 2773 Carmen Avenue
> Livermore, CA 94550

<u>Do not sign the original,</u> but don't forget to sign the copies before you mail them.

2773 Carmen Avenue
Livermore, California 94550
Telephone: 510 443 4327

Please accept this letter and my resumé as an expressed interest in joining your organization where my education and experience can be immediately and profitably utilized to our mutual benefit.

I believe that my background, knowledge and experience will enable me to contribute to your high standards, and I am confident I could provide many valuable contributions to your organization's work, and shall welcome the opportunity to discuss this with you in person.

If I can provide any additional information, or should you desire to arrange an interview, please contact me at my home address or telephone at your earliest convenience.

Thank you for your time and courtesy in reviewing this material and for your forthcoming response.

Sincerely,

Jack W. Wright
Enclosure:

SHIRLEY A. WRIGHT

2773 Carmen Avenue
Livermore, California 94550
Telephone: 510 443 4327

Please accept this letter and my resumé as an expressed interest in joining your organization where my education and experience can be immediately and profitably utilized to our mutual benefit.

I made a heartfelt decision to take time from my career to raise my children and further my education. Having completed this, I am now ready to return to my career. I am confident I could provide many valuable contributions to your organization's work, and shall welcome the opportunity to discuss this with you in person.

If I can provide any additional information, or should you desire to arrange an interview, please contact me at my home address or telephone at your earliest convenience.

Thank you for your time and courtesy in reviewing this material and for your forthcoming response.

Sincerely,

Shirley A. Wright
Enclosure:

THE FOLLOW-UP LETTER

Some say that the follow-up letter (sample on next Page) should be sent within 48 hours, and some say it should be mailed the same day as the interview. Some say it should be typed, and some say that handwritten is the best because it's more personal. Your letter will be personalized either way because you will be choosing your own words for this one. I show what each paragraph should contain, but the words are up to you.

If the manager you interviewed with seemed to be a formal sort of person, you will probably feel more confident if your letter is typewritten. If the interviewer seemed to be the "warm and friendly" type, you might want to write it by hand. If you do, please take the time to be sure that it's legible.

The sample follow-up letter is written on the assumption that you want the job. Most people don't write a follow-up letter unless they want the job (managers and high-profile individuals are the exception). If you want to tell them that you're not interested, you could write something in the second paragraph like, "It is with much regret that I must withdraw my candidacy from your consideration. I don't believe we are a good match for each other."

If you would like to be considered for some other position within the same company, you might use the same paragraph to say, "I would very much like to be considered for employment in another position (or area) that better matches my skills and interests."

Not everyone feels the need to send a follow-up letter, but if you really want the job, you should write one. Let's pretend for a moment that you are the hiring manager. You have just finished interviewing three candidates and are trying to select one. You like them equally, and they are all qualified and willing to start for the same salary. While you're trying to make your decision you receive a courteous, professional letter from one of the candidates. Now, who are you going to hire?

The follow-up letter is one of the least used and most important employment tools. USE IT!!!

JACK W. WRIGHT

2773 Carmen Avenue
Livermore, California 94550
Telephone: 510 443 4327

(Date)

Company Name
Name of Interviewer
Street or PO Address
City, State & Zip

Dear _____:

1st Paragraph: Thank the interviewer and express appreciation for the courtesy and consideration extended to you. Mention the position for which you interviewed, the date of the interview, and where the interview was conducted.

2nd Paragraph: Confirm your interest in the job. Mention anything you feel is important that you might have forgotten in the interview, and make up for any questions you didn't answer completely during the interview (we all think of something we forgot, or could have said better after we left).

3rd Paragraph: State that you're willing to provide any additional information, and add any further data you want to include on your application.

4th Paragraph: Close with a suggestion for further action or that you will be available for additional interviews at their convenience.

Sincerely,

Your Name

OPTICALLY SCANNABLE SAMPLE RESUMES

JACK W. WRIGHT

2773 Carmen Avenue
Livermore, California 94550
Telephone: 510 443 4327

ACCOUNTING/BOOKKEEPING

Available to discuss a challenging and responsible position
where my education and experience can be fully
utilized to our mutual benefit.

Summary of Skills

......experienced in bookkeeping and accounting......accounts payable......accounts receivable.....computer based accounting systems....credit and collections....10-key by touch....office management.....data entry.....balancing statements....payroll..... reconciliations....statistics.....billings.....staff supervision and training....developing work flow systems...excellent communication skills...ability to work under pressure ....able to interface well with all levels of management and personnel....reliable....... professional....

PROFESSIONAL HIGHLIGHTS

Physical Therapy Associates   1989 to Present
San Ramon, California
Bookkeeper
Position responsibilities include maintaining patient, insurance company, and physical therapist billing database and generating billings by inputting data into billing system. Duties include the following:
- Posting payments to receivable journal and customer accounts, and maintaining current balances in Marathon Software.
- Supervision of collections and resolving disputes with insurance companies.
- Processing and maintaining vendor ledgers, scheduling payments, and maintaining company checking account.
- Reconciling statements and analyzing and reconciling subsidiary ledgers.
- Preparing journal entries, accounts payable reconciliation, and monitoring closings.
- Bank deposits and preparing documents to be processed by data entry group.
- Preparing and utilizing periodic financial reports, auditing monthly cost journal, and compiling daily financial information.

Accomplishments: Organized and implemented an efficient work flow system that resulted in significant cost savings.

Spreckels Sugar Company   1987 -1989
Pleasanton, California
Customer Service Rep.

STRENGTHS

Career reflects hard work, attention to detail, and the ability to meet exact specifications as well as cost, quality, safety and time objectives.

REFERENCES EXCELLENT AND AVAILABLE UPON REQUEST

JACK W. WRIGHT
2773 Carmen Avenue
Livermore, California 94550
Telephone: 510 443 4327

ACCOUNTING / GENERAL OFFICE
Available to discuss a challenging and responsible position
where my education and experience can be fully
utilized to our mutual benefit.

Summary of Skills

.....formal education.....experienced in all areas of accounting.....computer based accounting systems....payroll....accounts payable and receivable....bookkeeping and accounting...balancing statements...credit and collections...10-key by touch....record keeping......customer relations and service......cash flow management......training employees...excellent communication skills...ability to work under pressure....pride in quality performance and achievement....ability to work well with all levels of management and personnel....reliable....professional....

PROFESSIONAL HIGHLIGHTS

Computerland Corporation   10 / 92 to 9/ 93
Pleasanton, California
Accounts Receivable

Position responsibilities include the following:

- Reconciling bank statements and accounts, and involvement with inventories in an auditing capacity.
- Performing preaudit of accounts payable files for conformity with company standards.
- Preparing journal entries, accounts payable reconciliation, and monitoring closings.
- Batching and balancing of checks for bank deposit, and preparing documents to be processed by data entry group.
- Handling accounts payable and receivable, payroll, bank reconciliation's, billings, collections, and preparing quarterly state and federal reports.

Velvet Turtle   1991 -1992
Pleasanton, California
Customer Service

EDUCATION
Graduated from Heald Business College, Computerized Accounting,
Hayward, California, 1990.

STRENGTHS
Ability to create and present an excellent image of the company and its services to customers, and to coordinate and communicate well with clientele and management at all levels and efficiently meet objectives.

REFERENCES EXCELLENT AND AVAILABLE UPON REQUEST

71

JACK W. WRIGHT
2773 Carmen Avenue
Livermore, California 94550
Telephone: 510 443 4327

ACCOUNTING / PAYROLL

Available to discuss a challenging and responsible position
where my education and experience can be fully
utilized to our mutual benefit.

Summary of Skills

......over 15 years experience in accounting and payroll......experienced in customer relations and service......balancing statements....accounts payable and receivable..... 10-Key by touch......computer based accounting systems......cash flow management ....data entry....office machines.....order entry......customer quotes......billing......staff supervision and training......purchasing......ability to work well with all levels of management and personnel.....pride in quality performance and achievement..... reliable....professional....

PROFESSIONAL HIGHLIGHTS

Allied-Signal Aerospace Company   1/ 93 - 3 / 93
Livermore, California
Account Clerk II
Temporary position at Lawrence Livermore Lab. Assigned to verify that all necessary data was transferred from an old system to a newer one.

Fluor Daniel Services   3/ 90 - 1/ 93
Livermore, California
Payroll Clerk
Responsible for processing the payroll for approximately 240 full-time and 75 part-time employees on a weekly basis. Also researched employees questions, balanced petty cash checking account, and reconciled hours with Plant Engineering.

Tracy Printers   5 / 80 - 1/ 90
Tracy, California
Office Manager

Responsibilities included:

* Retail bookkeeping, managing and depositing cash, calculating account adjustments, and preparing refunds. inventories in an auditing capacity.
* Handling accounts payable and receivable, payroll, bank reconciliation's, billings, collections, and preparing state tax reports.

STRENGTHS

Ability to create and present an excellent image of the company and its services to customers, and to coordinate and communicate well with clientele and management at all levels and efficiently meet objectives.

REFERENCES EXCELLENT AND AVAILABLE UPON REQUEST

JACK W. WRIGHT
2773 Carmen Avenue
Livermore, California 94550
Telephone: 510 443 4327

ADMINISTRATION

Available to discuss a challenging and responsible position
where my education and experience can be fully
utilized to our mutual benefit.

Summary of Skills

....formal education....experienced in all areas of administration...data entry....filing.....
10-Key by touch.......planning and scheduling.......monthly cost reports.....procurement
financial management....office machines....heavy phone interface.....correspondence....
contracts......travel arrangements......providing support......computerized systems......
customer service and relations....training employees....excellent communication skills.....
pride in quality performance and achievement.......ability to work well with all levels of
management and personnel....reliable....professional....

PROFESSIONAL HIGHLIGHTS

Lawrence Livermore National Laboratory   10/ 81 to Present
Livermore, California
Administrative Specialist (2/ 93 to Present)

Responsible for supporting two Resource Managers. Duties include:

· Keyboarding and editing of technical and non-technical reports, letters, internal memos, and
  miscellaneous documents.
· Answering phones and inquiries, scheduling and arranging meetings, and coordinating
  conferences.
· Processing paperwork for visits and making foreign and domestic travel arrangements.
· Updating database files, preparing time cards, and preparing material for viewgraph
  presentations.
· Monitoring cost reports and resolving discrepancies, and handling all procurement actions.
Accomplishments: Received letter of commendation for the quality and consistency of my
performance.

Precision Engineering Program
Administrative Specialist IV (10 / 81 - 2/ 93)

EDUCATION

AA Degree in General Education, Las Positas Community College *
* Will complete in 1996.

STRENGTHS

Ability to create and present an excellent image of the company and its services to customers,
and to coordinate and communicate well with clientele and management at all levels and
efficiently meet objectives.

REFERENCES EXCELLENT AND AVAILABLE UPON REQUEST

JACK W. WRIGHT

2773 Carmen Avenue
Livermore, California 94550
Telephone: 510 443 4327

AIR CONDITIONING SERVICE TECHNICIAN

Available to discuss a challenging and responsible position
where my education and experience can be fully
utilized to our mutual benefit.

Summary of Skills

.....experienced in air conditioning systems....package units....built up systems....split systems...variable air volume units....chillers, DX and centrifugal....installation and maintenance of pneumatic control systems....trimax energy management systems...gas fired boilers and heating equipment customer relations and service.....ability to work well with all levels of management and personnel....reliable....competent....

PROFESSIONAL HIGHLIGHTS

Peninsula Air Conditioning   11/ 87 to Present
San Jose, California
A/C Service Technician
Position responsibilities include the service and repair of H.V.A.C. equipment, pneumatic and electronic controls, installation of pneumatic V.A.V. systems, refrigeration, piping, etc.. Was also responsible for customer relations and service.

Western Allied Service   8/ 84 - 11/ 87
Menlo Park, California
A/C Service Technician
Duties included the service and repair of H.V.A.C. equipment.

Air Systems, Inc.   6 / 83 - 7/ 84
San Jose, California
A/C Service Technician

EDUCATION

Completed Classes in General Education,
Las Positas Community College, Livermore, California

STRENGTHS

Ability to create and present an excellent image of the company and its services to customers, and to coordinate and communicate well with clientele and management at all levels and efficiently meet objectives.

REFERENCES EXCELLENT AND AVAILABLE UPON REQUEST

JACK W. WRIGHT
2773 Carmen Avenue
Livermore, California 94550
Telephone: 510 443 4327
AIRCRAFT MECHANIC
Available to discuss a challenging and responsible position
where my education and experience can be fully
utilized to our mutual benefit.

Summary of Skills

....formal education....experienced in powerplants and airframes....troubleshooting and repair......tracking aircraft and engine equipment.......scheduled and unscheduled maintenance.....safety and performance modifications.....coordinating repairs....gas turbine and reciprocal engines.....checks and overhauls.....inspections.....quality control ....fuel systems....documentation and reports....bilingual, fluent in English and Spanish ....excellent communication skills....ability to work well with all levels of management and personnel......pride in quality performance and achievement......reliable..... professional...

PROFESSIONAL HIGHLIGHTS

U.S. Air Force Reserve   1993 to Present
Jet Engine Mechanic
Types of aircraft include C-141's with TF-33's, and C5A's with TF-39's.   Position responsibilities include the following:
- Performing scheduled and unscheduled maintenance, and safety/performance modifications.
- Training personnel in scheduling, tracking, coordinating, researching and updating the mainframe.
- Troubleshooting, removal and replacement of all components in the powerplant system.
- Familiar with the use of A/C manuals in reading schematics and researching difficulties.
- Supervision of personnel on Time Change Technical Orders, Hourly Time Change Items, and scheduling maintenance.

Hexcel Corporation   2/ 87 - 9/ 93
Livermore, California
In-Process Control Technician

EDUCATION
Completed Air Force Schools for Jet Engine Technician and
Organizational Maintenance.

STRENGTHS
Career reflects hard work, attention to detail, and the ability to meet exact specifications as well as cost, quality, safety and time objectives.

REFERENCES EXCELLENT AND AVAILABLE UPON REQUEST

JACK W. WRIGHT
2773 Carmen Avenue
Livermore, California 94550
Telephone: 510 443 4327

ARCHITECT

Available to discuss a challenging and responsible position
where my education and experience can be fully
utilized to our mutual benefit.

Summary of Skills

.....formal education....experienced in site and master planning studies....floor plans ....elevation studies...details and construction documents...presentation drawings.... special layouts......model studies......working with clients and subcontractors...... excellent communication skills....pride in quality performance and achievement.... ability to work well with all levels of management and personnel......reliable...... professional....

PROFESSIONAL HIGHLIGHTS

Acme Associates   1989 to Present
San Jose, California
Designer

Position responsibilities include site plan studies for:

- Bishop Rancy - 15 office complex, San Ramon California. This included floor plans and elevations.
- Gagos / Mosdesto Business Park, Modesto, California
- Beazer / Mountain View Office Park, Mountain View, California.
- Town House Development, Menlo Park, California.
- Details / Construction Documents - for Chateau Duvallon - a private 18,000 square foot private estate.

EDUCATION

Bachelor of Architecture, Kansas State University.
Foreign Study, School of Architecture, Aarhus, Denmark.
Construction Drafting, Phoenix, Arizona.

Work Experience

Evaluation and Programming Research; Seaton Hall, KSU Campus.
Assistant to Dean and Head of Department of Architecture.
Schematic Design Work for St. Mary's City Hall, Kansas.
Construction, Maintenance, and Sales at the Thunderbird Marina, Milford Lake,
and Junction City, Kansas.

STRENGTHS

Creative and energetic, capable of the sustained effort necessary to see a project through from conception to completion.

REFERENCES EXCELLENT AND AVAILABLE UPON REQUEST

JACK W. WRIGHT
2773 Carmen Avenue
Livermore, California 94550
Telephone: 510 443 4327

ASSEMBLER / OPERATOR

Available to discuss a challenging and responsible position
where my education and experience can be fully
utilized to our mutual benefit.

Summary of Skills

....formal education....experienced in operating wafer fab production equipment..... electronic assembly.....troubleshooting and repair.....soldering.....quality assurance ....microscopes....familiar with schematics and blueprints....coordinating equipment with production schedules....rework.....computers and software....staff supervision and training......excellent communication skills.....pride in quality performance and achievement....ability to work well with all levels of management and personnel.... reliable....professional....

PROFESSIONAL HIGHLIGHTS

Endosonics Corporation   1992 to Present
Pleasanton, California
Assembler
Position responsibilities include electronic assembly, testing, and quality control of complex medical equipment.

Intel Corporation   1987 -1992
Livermore, California
Plasma Operator
Duties included a wide variety of manufacturing operations in the Plasma Area, and was a member of the self-managing work team involved in setting daily priorities.
Accomplishments:
· Received Back to Basics awards for detecting defects in equipment and wafers.
· Received quarterly cash bonuses for perfect attendance.
· 100% qualified on D&W Oxide, Plasma Ashers, I P C Etchers, Hard Bake, Microscope, Resist Check, Wet Stations, and Tencor Machine.

EDUCATION

Completed Classes in Computers and Software Applications,
Las Positas Community College, Livermore, California

STRENGTHS

Career reflects hard work, attention to detail, and the ability to meet exact specifications as well as cost, quality, safety and time objectives.

REFERENCES EXCELLENT AND AVAILABLE UPON REQUEST

77

JACK W. WRIGHT
2773 Carmen Avenue
Livermore, California 94550
Telephone: 510 443 4327

AUTO MECHANIC / SERVICE MANAGER
Available to discuss a challenging and responsible position
where my education and experience can be fully
utilized to our mutual benefit.

Summary of Skills

.....formal training.....over 19 years experience.....experienced in all areas of automotive repair....management and supervision....customer relations and service.... training employees....working with vendors....computerized operations....hiring and firing....quality control....planning and scheduling....job costing....scheduling staff...reports and documentation...excellent communication skills...pride in quality performance and achievement....ability to work well with all levels of management and personnel...reliable...professional....

PROFESSIONAL HIGHLIGHTS

Precision Auto Repair   1983 to Present
Pleasanton, California
Shop Foreman
Position responsibilities include the following:

- Conducting customer transactions in a friendly, courteous, and expedient manner.
- Accurate performance of all computerized operations necessary for customer transactions.
- Insuring prompt service, resolving customer problems, cash management, and handling paperwork.
- Repairing and maintenance of chassis, brake systems, transmissions, clutches, and electrical and hydraulic systems.
- Major repairs, and tune-up of gasoline engines utilizing computerized test equipment.
- Performing D O T inspections in accordance with company policies and guidelines.

EDUCATION
Completed Numerous Factory Sponsored Training Classes

STRENGTHS

Career reflecting total involvement, high motivation, persuasive interaction and communication with people, eagerness to work, and proven leadership qualities.

REFERENCES EXCELLENT AND AVAILABLE UPON REQUEST

JACK W. WRIGHT
2773 Carmen Avenue
Livermore, California 94550
Telephone: 510 443 4327

AUTOMOTIVE PAINTER

Available to discuss a challenging and responsible position
where my education and experience can be fully
utilized to our mutual benefit.

Summary of Skills

.....formal training.....experienced in all areas of auto body painting....all types of paint and painting procedures...various spray guns...familiar with all standard tools ....prepping surfaces..sanding techniques...masking and detail work....mixing paints ....matching colors....quality control....customer relations and service....training employees....working with vendors......computerized operations......job costing..... planning and scheduling......excellent communication skills......pride in quality performance and achievement....ability to work well with all levels of management and personnel...reliable...professional....

PROFESSIONAL HIGHLIGHTS

Precision Auto Repair   1989 to Present
Pleasanton, California
Lead Painter

Position responsibilities include the following:

- Preparing automobiles for painting by block sanding, masking, and applying primer.
- Prepping, sanding, minor body work, detailing, mixing paints, matching colors, and spraying.
- Insuring prompt service, resolving customer problems, cash management, and handling paperwork.

Crown Chevrolet   1985 - 1989
Dublin, California
Apprentice Painter

EDUCATION
Completed Numerous Factory Sponsored Schools in
Automotive Painting and Repair.

STRENGTHS
Career reflecting total involvement, high motivation, persuasive interaction and communication with people, eagerness to work, and proven leadership qualities.

REFERENCES EXCELLENT AND AVAILABLE UPON REQUEST

JACK W. WRIGHT

2773 Carmen Avenue
Livermore, California 94550
Telephone: 510 443 4327

BOOKKEEPER

Available to discuss a challenging and responsible position
where my education and experience can be fully
utilized to our mutual benefit.

Summary of Skills

....formal education....experienced in full service accounting and tax preparation.... accounts payable and receivable....credit approvals and collections.....monthly tax and PUC reports....computerized accounting systems....10 Key by touch....customer relations and service......balancing statements.....staff supervision and training..... filing......excellent communication skills.....pride in quality performance and achievement....ability to work well with all levels of management and personnel.... reliable....professional....

PROFESSIONAL HIGHLIGHTS

Larson's Classic Oak   1992 - 1993
Livermore, California
Bookkeeper
Position responsibilities included bookkeeping, customer service, computers, bank reconciliation's, banking, and heavy phone interface.

Key Management   1981 - 1991
Salem, Oregon
Accountant
Responsible for full service accounting and tax preparation. Duties included:
· Reconciling bank statements and accounts, and involvement with inventories in an auditing capacity.
· Maintaining the accounts of 28 partnerships and 7 corporations.
· Handling accounts payable and receivable, bank reconciliation's, billings, collections, and preparing quarterly state and federal reports.
· Batching and balancing of checks for bank deposit, and preparing documents to be processed by data entry group.

EDUCATION

AA Degree in Accounting, Portland Community College,
Portland, Oregon. Honor Student - GPA 3.5

STRENGTHS

Career reflects hard work, attention to detail, and the ability to meet exact specifications as well as cost, quality, safety and time objectives.

REFERENCES EXCELLENT AND AVAILABLE UPON REQUEST

JACK W. WRIGHT
2773 Carmen Avenue
Livermore, California 94550
Telephone: 510 443 4327

CHEF/ ASSISTANT CHEF

Available to discuss a challenging and responsible position
where my education and experience can be fully
utilized to our mutual benefit.

Summary of Skills

......formal education.....experienced in kitchen operations and food preparation...... cost and quality control....menu planning....ordering food and supplies....safety and sanitation.....customer relations and service.....staff supervision and training.....cash flow management.....excellent communication skills.....pride in quality performance and achievement.....ability to work well with all levels of management and personnel....reliable....professional....

PROFESSIONAL HIGHLIGHTS

United States Navy   7/ 70 - 4 / 93
San Francisco, California
Chef / Kitchen Supervisor (E-7)

Position responsibilities include the following:

- Insuring prompt delivery of food, resolving customer problems, closing out cash receipts, and handling paperwork.
- Scheduling employees, insuring customer satisfaction, closing out cash receipts, completing required paperwork, and supervising the preparation of the main dining room.
- Kitchen operations, ordering food and supplies, menu planning, and quality control.
- Working with the Food Director regarding menu research and specifications, and training restaurant personnel.
- Kitchen operations, hiring, training, cost and quality control in serving lunch, dinner, brunch and banquets.
- Menu development and product specifications for lunch and dinners, banquets, brunch and buffets. Complete control of kitchen operations and supervision of staff.

Accomplishments: Received numerous commendations for the quality and consistency of my performance.

EDUCATION

AA Degree in General Education, Chabot Community College. *
* Will Graduate in 1996

STRENGTHS

Ability to create and present an excellent image of the company and its services to customers, and to coordinate and communicate well with clientele and management at all levels and efficiently meet objectives.

REFERENCES EXCELLENT AND AVAILABLE UPON REQUEST

JACK W. WRIGHT

2773 Carmen Avenue
Livermore, California 94550
Telephone: 510 443 4327

CREDIT MANAGER

Available to discuss a challenging and responsible position
where my education and experience can be fully
utilized to our mutual benefit.

Summary of Skills

......formal training.....experienced in credit and collections....financial management.... customer relations and service......policies and procedures......staff supervision and training....contracts.....assessing customer needs.....computerized operations...... people handling skills....analyzing....problem solving....record keeping....reports.....analyzing..... ability to work well with all levels of management and personnel.....reliable...... professional....

PROFESSIONAL HIGHLIGHTS

First National Credit Bureau   4 / 84 to Present
San Francisco, California
Manager, Credit & Collections
Position includes administrative responsibility for a staff of 12 personnel.   Duties include the following:

- Performing all aspects of credit and collection as required by the Chairman of the Board and the President of the Domestic Collection Agency.
- Direct involvement in goal setting strategy for successful financial management.
- Structuring .and performing all procedures relative to and necessary for the improvement of cash flow and the reduction of past due dollars.
- Interfacing with division heads in the coordination of procedures for new and existing accounts.
- Accomplishments: Assisted in company wide implementation of cedit procedures.
- Was Leading collector for most of a 25 month period.

EDUCATION

Dun & Bradstreet Financial Analysis Course, Leadership Course, Methods of Organizational Changes, Managing the Investment in Receivables, and the Effective Supervision of People.

STRENGTHS

Expert organizer and energetic, aggressive communicator with a proven ability to accomplish the most detailed, sensitive activity while remaining within the prescribed policy.

REFERENCES EXCELLENT AND AVAILABLE UPON REQUEST

JACK W. WRIGHT

2773 Carmen Avenue
Livermore, California 94550
Telephone: 510 443 4327

COMPUTER PROGRAMMER

Available to discuss a challenging and responsible position
where my education and experience can be fully
utilized to our mutual benefit.

Summary of Skills

......formal education......over 6 years experience in computer programming...... experienced in VAX BASIC...VERSACAD CPL....FORTRAN....COBOL....Pascal....systems include DEC......Hewlett-Packard......IBM.....Apple.....Pyramid.....Cyber.....Control Data.... experienced in systems management......reports......analyzing.....staff supervision and training......reports......excellent communication skills......ability to work under pressure.... ability to work well with all levels of management and personnel.... reliable....professional....

PROFESSIONAL HIGHLIGHTS

Triad Systems, Inc.   7/ 88 to Present
Livermore, California
Computer Programmer
Position responsibilities includes computer programming in VAX BASIC and VAX / VMS using DEC VAX / VMS and VERSACAD CPL using MS-DOS.

Account Temps Agency   1/ 88 - 7/ 88
Pleasanton, California
Temporary
Duties included Data Entry and Computer Programming for various companies in different environments and conditions.

Atlas Construction   1987 - 1988
Oakland, California
Systems Manager
Responsible for bringing system back on lineas needed when problems occurred.

EDUCATION

BS Degree in Computer Science, Cal State University
Hayward, California
Completed Classes in Computer Science and Math, Chabot Jr. College.

STRENGTHS

Expert organizer and energetic, aggressive communicator with a proven ability to accomplish the most detailed, sensitive activity while remaining within the prescribed policy.

REFERENCES EXCELLENT AND AVAILABLE UPON REQUEST

JACK W. WRIGHT
2773 Carmen Avenue
Livermore, California 94550
Telephone: 510 443 4327

CONSTRUCTION

Available to discuss a challenging and responsible position
where my education and experience can be fully
utilized to our mutual benefit.

Summary of Skills

......formal education......over 15 years experience......journeyman carpenter...... experienced in customer service and relations......customer warranty service......reading blueprints......all phases of construction....working with subcontractors....estimations and bids...building codes and permits....interfacing with develpers, contractors and the public....problem solving.....excellent communication skills......ability to work under pressure......ability to work well with all levels of management and personnel....reliable....competent.....professional....

PROFESSIONAL HIGHLIGHTS

L & D Construction, Inc.   8/ 91 to Present
Livermore, California
Journeyman Carpenter
Responsible for inspection and troubleshooting completed construction to resolve customer problems. Duties include:
- Constructing single family and multifamily residential buildings.
- Working closely with architects, vendors, and city building department, and obtaining sewer and building permits.
- Scheduling personnel and coordinating production schedule to complete projects in a timely and cost effective manner.

Nance Concrete and Construction   2/ 90 - 8/ 91
Hayward, California
Pick-up Carpenter
Duties included supervising crews in all phases of construction and interacting with subcontractors.

EDUCATION
BA Degree in Sociology, University of Washington.
AA Degree in General Education, Las Positas College,
Livermore, California.

STRENGTHS

Multiplicity of experience and skills including carpentry, wood work, metals, plumbing, mechanics, and general maintenance and repair.

REFERENCES EXCELLENT AND AVAILABLE UPON REQUEST

JACK W. WRIGHT
2773 Carmen Avenue
Livermore, California 94550
Telephone: 510 443 4327

CONTRACTS ADMINISTRATOR

Available to discuss a challenging and responsible position
where my education and experience can be fully
utilized to our mutual benefit.

Summary of Skills

......formal education.......experienced in the construction industry......contracts...... proposals....budget preparation.....policies and procedures.....corporate liaison...... program and plan implementation....negotiations....staff supervision and training ....purchasing....working with vendors....job costing....computerized systems....cost estimations....reports....people handling skills.....ability to work under pressure..... ability to work well with all levels of management and personnel.....reliable...... competent... professional....

PROFESSIONAL HIGHLIGHTS

Public Storage Co.   1984 to Present
Livermore, California
Contract Administrator
Position responsibilities include extensive administration of contracts with numerous subcontractors. Duties include:
· Selection of subcontractors, plan implementation, and liaison with various project engineers, scheduling project completion time, and reviewing and evaluating plans and suggesting modifications for on going and future projects.
· Reviewing and upgrading of project specifications.
· Preparing final budgets with regional construction managers, and administration of from 5 to 9 projects simultaneously.
· Assist in selecting project superintendents, evaluating extra work requests, and determining progress payments for subcontractors.

Balboa Engineers   1979 - 1984
Hayward, California
Estimator
Assisted in scheduling and supervising the work of employees and assisted with field work as required.

EDUCATION
BS Degree in Civil Engineering, California State University.
Completed Classes in Computer Programming and Real Estate.

STRENGTHS

Expert organizer and energetic, aggressive communicator with a proven ability to accomplish the most detailed, sensitive activity while remaining within the prescribed policy.

REFERENCES EXCELLENT AND AVAILABLE UPON REQUEST

JACK W. WRIGHT
2773 Carmen Avenue
Livermore, California 94550
Telephone: 510 443 4327

CONVENIENCE STORE MANAGER

Available to discuss a challenging and responsible position
where my education and experience can be fully
utilized to our mutual benefit.

Summary of Skills

.....formal education.....experienced in retail sales......staff supervision and training...... merchandising....inventory control....purchasing......working with vendors......customer relations and service....hiring and firing....creating displays....implementing policies and procedures....hard working....computerized systems.....excellent communication skills.... ability to work under pressure.....ability to work well with all levels of management and personnel....reliable....competent....professional....

PROFESSIONAL HIGHLIGHTS

Arco AM / PM Mini Market   1981 to Present
Livermore, California
Manager / Cashier
Position responsibilities include:
· Training and supervision of 8 staff members.
· Establishing long and short term goals and plans.
· Hiring and firing, establishing and revising store policies, and bookkeeping.
· Inventory control, buying, merchandising, and retail sales.
· Maintenance and compliance with city, county, state and federal regulations.

Patterson Pacific Parchment Co.   1979 - 1981
Sunnyvale, California
Warehouseman
Responsibilities included loading and unloading of trucks and boxcars, filling orders, and maintaining large quantities of warehouse stock. Also participated in inventory control and operated a fork lift.

EDUCATION

Graduated Amador High School, Pleasanton, California.
Completed Classes in General Education, Las Positas College.

STRENGTHS

Ability to create and present an excellent image of the company and its services to customers, and to coordinate and communicate well with clientele and management at all levels and efficiently meet objectives.

REFERENCES EXCELLENT AND AVAILABLE UPON REQUEST

JACK W. WRIGHT
2773 Carmen Avenue
Livermore, California 94550
Telephone: 510 443 4327

CUSTODIAN / JANITOR

Available to discuss a challenging and responsible position
where my education and experience can be fully
utilized to our mutual benefit.

Summary of Skills

.....over 6 years of janitorial experience.....experienced in all phases of cleaning......light maintenance.....working with chemicals......mixing cleaning solutions and compounds......cleaning various floor surfaces....stripping and waxing....safety and operation of cleaning machines and equipment....maintaining interior and exterior lighting....material handling....maintaining stock levels....planning and scheduling... customer relations.....ability to work well with all levels of management and personnel.....reliable......competent.....professional....

PROFESSIONAL HIGHLIGHTS

Tri-Valley Manufacturing   1987 to Present
Livermore, California
Janitor / Assistant Helper
Responsible for custodial work and light maintenance. Duties include:
· Effectively prioritizing and organizing work loads in a constantly changing environment to meet daily and weekly schedules.
· Monitoring inventory levels and stock status to maintain a minimum supply level while insuring availability of cleaning supplies.
· Safe operation of various equipment used in the cleaning and protection of various floor surfaces and coverings.
· Daily inspection and auditing of facilities to maintain compliance with company standards.
Accomplishments: Commended by management on numerous occasions for the quality and consistency of my performance.

Patterson Pacific Parchment Co.   1983 - 1987
Sunnyvale, California
Warehouseman

EDUCATION
Graduated Amador High School, Pleasanton, California.

STRENGTHS
Ability to create and present an excellent image of the company and its services to customers, and to coordinate and communicate well with clientele and management at all levels and efficiently meet objectives.

REFERENCES EXCELLENT AND AVAILABLE UPON REQUEST

JACK W. WRIGHT

2773 Carmen Avenue
Livermore, California 94550
Telephone: 510 443 4327

CUSTOMER SERVICE

Available to discuss a challenging and responsible position
where my education and experience can be fully
utilized to our mutual benefit.

Summary of Skills

....formal education...experienced in customer relations and service.....computerized systems...software....assessing customer needs....inventory control....data entry....typing .....heavy phone interface.....office machines......pricing......merchandising......customer quotes....outside sales.....order entry......departmental liaison......record keeping..... working with vendors.....shipping and receiving......reports.....ability to work under pressure....creative problem solving....excellent communication skills....pride in quality performance and achievement......ability to work well with all levels of management and personnel....reliable....professional....

PROFESSIONAL HIGHLIGHTS

Computerland Corp.   1991 - 12/ 93
Pleasanton, California
Customer Service Representative

Position responsibilities include the following:

- Conducting customer transactions in a friendly, courteous, and expedient manner.
- Accurate performance of all computerized operations necessary for customer transactions.
- Insuring customer satisfaction by resolving customer complaints.
- Effectively prioritizing and organizing work loads in a constantly changing environment to meet schedules.
- Performing work with minimal direction and establishing priorities on a daily basis.
- Typing invoice entries, releasing back orders, and sorting and filing invoices.

Kelly Temporary Services   9/ 90 - 12/ 91
Pleasanton, California
Customer Service Rep.

EDUCATION

AA Degree in Business Administration, Las Positas College. *
* Will graduate in 1996.

STRENGTHS

Ability to create and present an excellent image of the company and its services to customers, and to coordinate and communicate well with clientele and management at all levels and efficiently meet objectives.

REFERENCES EXCELLENT AND AVAILABLE UPON REQUEST

JACK W. WRIGHT
2773 Carmen Avenue
Livermore, California 94550
Telephone: 510 443 4327

DATA ENTRY

Available to discuss a challenging and responsible position
where my education and experience can be fully
utilized to our mutual benefit.

Summary of Skills

..formal education....experienced in word processing and data entry....experienced with Wang, IBM, & Apple word processing systems....filing....ten-key....key punch ...training employees...heavy phone interface...office machines...customer relations and service.....order entry.....record keeping......reports......ability to work under pressure ....creative problem solving....excellent communication skills.....pride in quality performance and achievement......ability to work well with all levels of management and personnel....reliable....professional....

PROFESSIONAL HIGHLIGHTS

Davionic Manufacturing   1987 to Present
Pleasanton, California
Data Entry Operator

Position responsibilities include the following:

- Accurately entering statistical data relating to engineering projects at various locations.
- Recording statistical data related to new applications, rewrites, endorsements, and cancellations.
- Determining additional handling required as advised by system and routing to the appropriate processing units.
- Effectively prioritizing and organizing work loads in a constantly changing environment to meet schedules.
- Performing work with minimal direction and establishing priorities on a daily basis.
- Typing invoice entries, releasing back orders, and sorting and filing invoices.

Tymshare   1985 - 1987
Pleasanton, California
Data Entry Operator

EDUCATION

BS Degree in Business, University of Phoenix, will complete next spring.
AA Degree in General Education, Chabot College.

STRENGTHS

Expert organizer and energetic, aggressive communicator with a proven ability to accomplish the most detailed, sensitive activity while remaining within the prescribed policy.

REFERENCES EXCELLENT AND AVAILABLE UPON REQUEST

JACK W. WRIGHT
2773 Carmen Avenue
Livermore, California 94550
Telephone: 510 443 4327

DENTAL ASSISTANT

Available to discuss a challenging and responsible position
where my education and experience can be fully
utilized to our mutual benefit.

Summary of Skills

.....formal education......experienced in RDA functions.....custom crown and bridge temporaries....construction of custom trays....nightguards....bleaching stints....implant stints....working with implant cases....soft tissue exams...orthodonics...fitting bands ....impressions....sterilization....X-ray license...assisting periodontists, oral surgeons, orthodontists, and endodontists.....computerized systems.....customer relations and service....scheduling appointments....phones and front office....keeping records.... excellent communication skills....ability to interface well with all levels of management and personnel....reliable....professional....

PROFESSIONAL HIGHLIGHTS

Charles Bocks III D.D.S.   1/ 93 to Present
San Jose, California
Registered Dental Assistant
Position responsibilities include providing chairside assistance, constructing custom trays, nightguards, bleaching stints, implant stints, and working with implant cases.

Piedmont Hills Dental Center   1981 - 1992
San Jose, California
Registered Chairside Assistant
· Assisting dentist, periodontists, oral surgeons, and orthodontists.
· RDA functions including soft tissue exams and crown and bridge temporaries.
· Excellent working knowledge of sterilization procedures.
· Working the front office, scheduling patients, and operation of companies computer system.

EDUCATION

Completed Classes in Administration, West Valley College
Certificate in CPR
Certificate in Radiation Safety

STRENGTHS

A dedicated professional with initiative, drive and the desire to excel, with patience, care, and a genuine desire to help people.

REFERENCES EXCELLENT AND AVAILABLE UPON REQUEST

JACK W. WRIGHT
2773 Carmen Avenue
Livermore, California 94550
Telephone: 510 443 4327

ELECTRICAL ENGINEER

Available to discuss a challenging and responsible entry level
position where my education and experience can be
fully utilized to our mutual benefit.

Summary of Skills

.....formal education.....experienced in computer architecture...hardware and software ...microelectronic circuits...digital and analog...data structures....circuit analysis and design...programming...signal processing...troubleshooting and repair...test equipment .....quality control.....inventory control.....documentation.....excellent communication skills...career desire...pride in quality performance and achievement ......ability to work well with all levels of management and personnel.....reliable....professional....

EDUCATION

BS Degree in Electrical Engineering
University of California at Davis, California, 1993

Coursework included:

- Circuit analysis and design, signal processing and analysis, digital systems, and filter design. Also courses in computer science that included computer architecture, operating systems, data structures, and various programming languages.
- Management science and engineering economics and courses related to the business side of engineering.

Projects included:

- Designed and implemented an analog and digital signal processing system.
- Designed a 4 bit multiplier using the algorithmic state machine method.
- Designed a memory system with a bi-directional 8 -bit data bus.

Computer skills:

- Word processing on MultiMate and WordPerfect.
- Programming in Pascal and C.
- Experience with UNIX, MINIX, VMS, and Windows.
- Experience with Spice and Matlab.

While Pursuing Education

Worked summers as a Test Assistant, Surveyor, Office Assistant, and Income Tax Processor.

Additional

Member of IEEE and participated in Public Relations

REFERENCES EXCELLENT AND AVAILABLE UPON REQUEST

JACK W. WRIGHT
2773 Carmen Avenue
Livermore, California 94550
Telephone: 510 443 4327

ELECTRONIC TECHNICIAN / ASSISTANT ENGINEER

Available to discuss a challenging and responsible position
where my education and experience can be fully
utilized to our mutual benefit.

Summary of Skills

...formal education...experienced in computer software and hardware....installation ....configuration....testing....system architechure....network management.....analog and digital....troubleshooting and repair....logic diagrams and schematics.....reports....staff supervision and training....documentation....excellent communication skills....pride in quality performance and achievement....ability to work well with all levels of management and personnel....reliable....professional....

PROFESSIONAL HIGHLIGHTS

Lawrence Livermore National Laboratory   1988 - 1993
Livermore, California
Electronics Technical Associate
Position responsibilities included managing and maintaining the open and closed networks and RISC - based UNIX computers deployed by CNC.   Duties included the following:

- Installation, configuration, testing and documentation of hardware and software.
- Effectively interact with management and developers to influence project priorities, system architecture, security, system performance and costs.
- Assisting with the development and implementation of computer configuration management and network management.

Accomplishments: Was commended by management on numerous occasions for the quality and consistency of my performance.

Lawrence Livermore National Laboratory   1983 - 1988
Livermore, California
Sr. Electronic Technician
Responsible for design and testing of diagnostic's to measure current and voltage on high voltage pulsed extractor for laser isotope separation.

EDUCATION

Completed Classes in General Education,
Las Positas Community College, Livermore, California

STRENGTHS

Career reflects hard work, attention to detail, and the ability to meet exact specifications as well as cost, quality, safety and time objectives.

REFERENCES EXCELLENT AND AVAILABLE UPON REQUEST

JACK W. WRIGHT
2773 Carmen Avenue
Livermore, California 94550
Telephone: 510 443 4327

ENGINEERING / MANUFACTURING

Available to discuss a challenging and responsible position
where my education and experience can be fully
utilized to our mutual benefit.

Summary of Skills

....formal education......experienced in all areas of engineering and manufacturing..... custom machines and tooling......project planning......contracts......proposals.....P & L responsibility......negotiations......staff supervision and training......preparing annual operating and capital expense equipment budgets......customer relations and service ....customer quotes....pricing.....sales and marketing.....excellent communication skills.... reports......abililty to work well with all levels of management and personnel...... professional....

PROFESSIONAL HIGHLIGHTS

ManuFax Engineering Corp.   1986 to Present
Livermore, California
Manager
Position responsibilities for this design facility and machine shop include:
- Designing, project planning, estimating, and production / material control.
- Quality control, inspection procedures, purchasing, and supervision of employees.
- Scheduling, coordinating, and organizing daily and monthly budget projects, and maintaining financial record systems.
- Effectively prioritizing and organizing work loads in a constantly changing environment to meet schedules.

Electrofusion Corp.   1984 - 1986
Fremont, California
Project Engineer

EDUCATION
BA Degree in General Education and Engineering, Cal State Hayward. *
* Will graduate spring of 1997.

Additional
Senior Member, Society of Manufacturing Engineers.
Certified Manufacturing Engineer

STRENGTHS
High professional level, excellence of leadership technique, and professional attention to detail supplemented by the ability to influence and stimulate others.

REFERENCES EXCELLENT AND AVAILABLE UPON REQUEST

JACK W. WRIGHT
2773 Carmen Avenue
Livermore, California 94550
Telephone: 510 443 4327

ENVIRONMENTAL TECHNOLOGIST

Available to discuss a challenging and responsible position
where my education and experience can be fully
utilized to our mutual benefit.

Summary of Skills

...formal education....experienced in handling radioactive materials....waste storage .....operating radiation survey instruments emergency and safety procedures...... decontamination procedures....quality control....computerized operations....reports and documentation....inventory control....material handling equipment....detail oriented.... creative problem solving....DOE 'Q' clearance....excellent communication skills....abililty to work well with all levels of management and personnel....professional....

PROFESSIONAL HIGHLIGHTS

Bendix Field Engineering Corp.   1986 to Present
Livermore, California
Sr. Systems Technician
Position responsibilities include numerous functions in the collection, packaging, labeling, identifying, segregating, storing, treating, and disposing of hazardous and radioactive waste products. Duties include:
- Handling radioactive / hazardous materials, developing quality control standards, and safety and EX & H responsibilities.
- Respirator custodian for materials testing laboratories. Up to date training in all essential courses.
- Development of efficiency QA / QC methods and records management procedures for tracking large numbers of critical components used in the construction of Uranium Separators.
- Decontamination and documenting pretest inspection and characterization procedures for critical uranium handling components.
- Fabrication and welding of vacuum plumbing systems for Uranium Separator.

EDUCATION

Completed Courses in Physics, Vacuum Technology and Welding,
Los Positas College.
Current with all ES&H training classes.

STRENGTHS

Capable of initial program development and handling liaison with governmental agencies, private sources, and community relations.

REFERENCES EXCELLENT AND AVAILABLE UPON REQUEST

94

JACK W. WRIGHT
2773 Carmen Avenue
Livermore, California 94550
Telephone: 510 443 4327

FIREFIGHTER

Available to discuss a challenging and responsible position
where my education and experience can be fully
utilized to our mutual benefit.

Summary of Skills

.......formal education.......over 10 years experience in firefighting........experienced in structural / wildland fires....firefighter I certificate # 016718....live fire training....EMT / 1A.....advanced first aid.....CPR certificate......emergency care....operation of emergency vehicles.....cardiopulmonary resuscitation.....vehicular extrication....ventilation methods and techniques...fire station maintenance....search and rescue....forcible entry....reports .....excellent communication skills.....ability to work well with all levels of management and personnel....reliable....professional....

PROFESSIONAL HIGHLIGHTS

Pleasanton Fire Department   1980 to Present
Pleasanton, California
Reserve Firefighting
Position responsibilities include active service as a reserve firefighter with the
Pleasanton Fire Department. Duties include the following:
- Rescuing endangered persons and property, operating engine pumps and using related apparatus.
- Extinguishing fires with water or chemicals, and administering emergency medical care.
- Maintaining fire station, engines, related grounds, facilities, equipment and supplies.
- Responding quickly to calls for a local second alarm, and attending reserve meetings and drill sessions.
- Participating in station events - Fire Safety, open house, and local Fire Prevention Programs.

Petrini Markets   1988 to Present
San Ramon, California
Assistant Produce Manager
Duties include merchandising, retail sales, customer service, inventory control, and training new employees in company procedures.

EDUCATION

AS Degree in Fire Science, Chabot Community College. *
* Will complete in 1996

STRENGTHS

Career reflecting total involvement, high motivation, persuasive interaction and communication with people, eagerness to work, and proven leadership qualities.

REFERENCES EXCELLENT AND AVAILABLE UPON REQUEST

JACK W. WRIGHT
2773 Carmen Avenue
Livermore, California 94550
Telephone: 510 443 4327

FITNESS INSTRUCTOR / PERSONAL TRAINER

Available to discuss a challenging and responsible position
where my education and experience can be fully
utilized to our mutual benefit.

Summary of Skills

.....formal education......experienced in all areas of physical training......designing fitness programs....nutrition....training staff and clients....excellent people handling skills....planning and scheduling.....developing exercise programs....physical therapy sports medicine...CPR certificate....advanced first aid certificate....customer relations and service.....ability to work under pressure.....cash flow management.....excellent communication skills......ability to work well with all levels of management and personnel...pride in quality and performance and achievement....reliable....

PROFESSIONAL HIGHLIGHTS

Schoebers Athletic Club   6 / 92 to Present
Pleasanton, California
Fitness Instructor

Position responsibilities include the following:

- Assisting members with their fitness needs and implementing a program specifically for their individual needs.
- Working with clients with previous injuries to help them return to normal activities.
- Conducting customer transactions in a friendly, courteous, and expedient manner.
- Accurate performance of all computerized operations necessary for customer transactions.
- Insuring prompt service, resolving customer problems, cash management, and handling paperwork.
- Insuring customer satisfaction by resolving customer complaints.
- Effectively prioritizing and organizing work loads in a constantly changing environment to meet schedules.
- Performing work with minimal direction and establishing priorities on a daily basis.

Accomplishments: Commended by my supervisor for the quality and consistency of my performance.

EDUCATION

AA Degree in Bio Dynamics, Las Positas Community College. *
* Will graduate in 1996.

STRENGTHS

Ability to create and present an excellent image of the company and its services to customers, and to coordinate and communicate well with clientele and management at all levels and efficiently meet objectives.

REFERENCES EXCELLENT AND AVAILABLE UPON REQUEST

JACK W. WRIGHT
2773 Carmen Avenue
Livermore, California 94550
Telephone: 510 443 4327

FOOD SERVICE

Available to discuss a challenging and responsible position
where my education and experience can be fully
utilized to our mutual benefit.

Summary of Skills

.....formal education.....experienced in all aspects of banquets and catering.....customer relations and service...staff supervision and training...hiring....scheduling...budgeting.... coordinating activities....maintaining records....employee relations...excellent...contracts communication skills....proposals....forecasting sales, profit, and expenses....scheduling staff......reports......able to work well under pressure......ability to work well with all levels of management and personnel...pride in quality performance and achievement.... professional....

PROFESSIONAL HIGHLIGHTS

Pleasanton Hilton   1987 to Present
Pleasanton, California
Banquet Captain
Responsible for working directly with the Catering Manager and event supervisors. Duties include the following:
- Scheduling employees, insuring customer satisfaction, closing out cash receipts, completing required paperwork, and supervising the preparation of all banquet meeting rooms.
- Working with the Banquet Manager regarding menu research and specifications, and training all banquet personnel.
- Effectively prioritizing and organizing work loads in a constantly changing environment to meet daily and weekly deadlines.
- Daily payroll, and breakdown of all food and beverage revenues.

Accomplishments: Commended by management on numerous occasions for the quality and consistency of my performance.

Sheraton Courtyard   1985 - 1987
Pleasanton, California
Lead Houseman

EDUCATION

Completed Classes in General Education,
Diablo Valley Community College, Pleasant Hill, California

STRENGTHS

Ability to create and present an excellent image of the company and its services to customers, and to coordinate and communicate well with clientele and management at all levels and efficiently meet objectives.

REFERENCES EXCELLENT AND AVAILABLE UPON REQUEST

JACK W. WRIGHT
2773 Carmen Avenue
Livermore, California 94550
Telephone: 510 443 4327

HEAVY EQUIPMENT OPERATOR / SURVEYOR

Available to discuss a challenging and responsible position
where my education and experience can be fully
utilized to our mutual benefit.

Summary of Skills

.....formal training....over 8 years experience in operating bulldozers, backhoes, scrapers and graders....experienced in minor and preventative maintenance.... rodman....chainman....shooting elevations....working with levels and transits.... Philadelphia and Lenker Rods....operating power tools....excellent communication skills....ability to well with all levels of management and personnel....pride in quality performance and achievement....professional....

PROFESSIONAL HIGHLIGHTS

Browning Farms, Inc.   1989 to Present
Livermore, California
Heavy Equipment Operator
Responsibilities at this landfill include:
- Operating Bulldozers, Scrapers, Compactors, Loaders and backhoes.
- Daily inspection of vehicles and performing preventative and light maintenance.
- Customer relations and service, and training new employees.

Depoali Equipment   1984 - 1989
Livermore, California
Heavy Equipment Operator
Company was taken over by Browning Farms; job responsibilities were the same as above.

EDUCATION

Graduate of Superior Training's Heavy Equipment Operators Course, Phoenix, Arizona. Coursework included:

Backhoes	**Bulldozers**
Case 580 C	Case 450
International 260	International TD7
Scrapers	**Graders**
Michigan	John Deere 570 & 570A
Michigan Clark	International Westinghouse
International	Fiat Atlas

STRENGTHS

Career reflects hard work, attention to detail, and the ability to meet exact specifications as well as cost, quality, safety and time objectives.

REFERENCES EXCELLENT AND AVAILABLE UPON REQUEST

JACK W. WRIGHT

2773 Carmen Avenue
Livermore, California 94550
Telephone: 510 443 4327

INVESTIGATOR

Available to discuss a challenging and responsible entry level
position where my education and experience can be
fully utilized to our mutual benefit.

Summary of Skills

.....formal education.....experienced in security.....customer relations and service.....
record keeping.....computerized systems......people handling skills......reports......
planning and scheduling.....analyzing.....problem solving.....training employees.....
ability to work under pressure.....excellent communication skills......ability to work well
with all levels of management and personnel....pride in quality performance and
achievement....reliable....professional....

PROFESSIONAL HIGHLIGHTS

Alameda County Sheriff's Department   1992 to Present
Santa Rita, California
Sheriff's Technician

Position responsibilities include the following:

- Developing and maintaining security and safety programs while keeping
  positive relations with all employees.
- Determining when security incidents are infractions and writing infraction
  reports when necessary.

Insurance Courier Services   1991 -1992
San Leandro, California
Courier
Duties included the driving and delivery of important documents, and per-
forming work with minimal direction and establishing priorities independently
on a daily basis.

EDUCATION

AA Degree in Administration of Justice,
Chabot Community College, Hayward, California

STRENGTHS

Ability to create and present an excellent image of the company and its services
to customers, and to coordinate and communicate well with clientele and
management at all levels and efficiently meet objectives.

REFERENCES EXCELLENT AND AVAILABLE UPON REQUEST

JACK W. WRIGHT
2773 Carmen Avenue
Livermore, California 94550
Telephone: 510 443 4327
LEGAL SECRETARY

Available to discuss a challenging and responsible entry level
position where my education and experience can be
fully utilized to our mutual benefit.

Summary of Skills

.....formal education.....customer relations and service......typing......data entry.....office machines....... computerized systems......10-Key.....accounts payable and receivable......heavy phone interface......staff supervision and training......word processing....billing ....developing work flow systems....record keeping.....reports....planning and scheduling ......analyzing.....problem solving......ability to work under pressure......excellent communication skills....pride in quality performance and achievement.....competent...... professional...

PROFESSIONAL HIGHLIGHTS

National Services, Inc.   1989 to Present
Pleasanton, California
Office Management
Position responsibilities include supervising a staff of four in the Administration Department. Duties include:
- Processing of all accounts payable and receivable, invoicing, and credit checks.
- Purchasing all office supplies and data entry.
- Interviewing, and hiring and firing of staff.

Accomplishments: Commended by management for the quality and consistency of my performance.

Grossman & Davis   1988 - 1989
Pleasanton, California
Legal Secretary
Duties included preparation of forms / pleadings; generating all correspondence; scheduling calendar appointments for follow ups and statutes; subpoenaed medical records; scheduled medical / legal appointments and conferences; client file evaluation, and back up for telephones.

EDUCATION
Legal Secretary Training Course, Castro Valley, California
Permanent Disability Rating Class, Oakland, California

STRENGTHS

Ability to create and present an excellent image of the company and its services to customers, and to coordinate and communicate well with clientele and management at all levels and efficiently meet objectives.

REFERENCES EXCELLENT AND AVAILABLE UPON REQUEST

JACK W. WRIGHT
2773 Carmen Avenue
Livermore, California 94550
Telephone: 510 443 4327

MAINTENANCE ENGINEER

Available to discuss a challenging and responsible position
where my education and experience can be fully
utilized to our mutual benefit.

Summary of Skills

....formal training....experienced in all areas of installation, maintenance, and repair of plant equipment.....welding, TIG and acetylene.....machine work.....radiation and hazardous materials....vacuum technology....staff supervision and training... drafting .....purchasing.....computerized systems.....quality control......familiar with prints, sketches, and schematics.....reports.....safety.....ability to work well with all levels of management and personnel......pride in quality performance and achievement..... reliable....professional....

PROFESSIONAL HIGHLIGHTS

Lawrence Livermore National Laboratory   1983 to Present
Livermore, California
Engineering Associate

Position responsibilities include the following:

- Maintenance and repair of pumps, compressors, bearings, and valves.
- Reading meters and gauges and making adjustments on manual or override controls to bring equipment to proper operating range.
- Maintenance and repair of hydraulics, pneumatics and water systems.
- Maintenance and repair of all building equipment, motors, and lighting circuits.
- Repair and overhaul of high vacuum pumps and systems, and repairs on piping and system components.
- Maintaining all operating equipment, reducing equipment down time, and installing new equipment.
- Maintenance and operation of plant projects, and maintaining spare parts inventory and supplies.
- Performing vendor surveys to find the highest quality parts for the lowest cost.
- Effectively prioritizing and organizing work loads in a constantly changing environment to meet schedules.

EDUCATION

Completed Numerous Company Sponsored Training Courses

STRENGTHS

Career reflects hard work, attention to detail, and the ability to meet exact specifications as well as cost, quality and time objectives.

REFERENCES EXCELLENT AND AVAILABLE UPON REQUEST

JACK W. WRIGHT
2773 Carmen Avenue
Livermore, California 94550
Telephone: 510 443 4327

MATERIALS / PURCHASING

Available to discuss a challenging and responsible position
where my education and experience can be fully
utilized to our mutual benefit.

Summary of Skills

......formal education......experienced in contracts......negotiations......purchasing...... logistics....inventory control....working with vendors....warehouse operations...... shipping and receiving....quality control....P & L responsiblity....office management ....staff supervision and training....computerized systems....collections and credit.... record keeping....reports....departmental liaison...excellent communication skills..... ability to work well with all levels of management.....pride in quality performance and achievement .....reliable....professional....

PROFESSIONAL HIGHLIGHTS

United Security Products   1983 to Present
Livermore, California
Materials Manager (11/ 89 to Present)
Responsibilities include management and supervision of the Purchasing Department,
Shipping and Receiving, and Stockroom. Duties include the following:
· Material procurement, vendor selection, and inventory control.
· Monitoring material flow form receipt to final product shipment.
· Liaison with Engineering on new product and new revision requirements.
· Resolution of quality and supply problems.
· Accuracy and turns ratio for raw material and finished goods inventory.
· Direction of daily production meetings.
 Accomplishments:
· Located and established offshore source for a major product component resulting in
  an annual savings of $130,000.

Purchasing Agent (10 / 84 - 11/ 89) Responsible for providing executive level
purchasing management and directing all materials procurement, inventory control,
and vendor selection.

EDUCATION
BA Degree in Business, UCLA.

STRENGTHS

Career reflects hard work, attention to detail, and the ability to meet exact
specifications as well as cost, quality and time objectives.

REFERENCES EXCELLENT AND AVAILABLE UPON REQUEST

JACK W. WRIGHT
2773 Carmen Avenue
Livermore, California 94550
Telephone: 510 443 4327

MEDICAL ASSISTANT

Available to discuss a challenging and responsible position
where my education and experience can be fully
utilized to our mutual benefit.

Summary of Skills

....formal education......experienced in staff supervision and training....patient relations and service....scheduling appointments...10-Key...filing...office machines...computerized operations....typing....keeping records....heavy phone interface....organizational skills.... excellent interpersonal and comunication skills.....office management......collections and credit.......ability to work well with all levels of management......pride in quality performance and achievement....reliable....professional....

PROFESSIONAL HIGHLIGHTS

East Bay E.N.T.   1986 to Present
Livermore, California
Medical Assistant
Responsibilities require familiarity with the use of standard medical test equipment and sterile techniques. Duties include:
· Taking patient's vital signs and medical history prior to doctor's consultation.
· Giving injections, taking EKG's, hearing tests, fitting custom ear molds, and ENG tests.

Crow Canyon Medical Center   1983 - 1986
San Ramon, California
Medical Assistant
Responsible for drawing blood and providing executive level purchasing management and directing all materials procurement, inventory control, and vendor selection.

EDUCATION
Medical Technical Data College, Certified Phlebotomy,
EKG Technician, and Lab Assistant. CPR certified.
Graduated November 1983.

STRENGTHS

Career reflects hard work, attention to detail, and the ability to meet exact specifications as well as cost, quality and time objectives.

REFERENCES EXCELLENT AND AVAILABLE UPON REQUEST

JACK W. WRIGHT
2773 Carmen Avenue
Livermore, California 94550
Telephone: 510 443 4327

OCCUPATIONAL HEALTH NURSE

Available to discuss a challenging and responsible position
where my education and experience can be fully
utilized to our mutual benefit.

Summary of Skills

.....formal education.....registered nurse......certified in CPR, ACLS, and NALS......
experienced in all phases of nursing, injections, medications, vital signs, IV skills,
maintaining patient records....medical / surgical.....labor and delivery......cardiac care,
including telemetry......staff supervision and training......excellent communication
skills...pride in quality performance and achievement....ability to work well with all
levels of management and personnel....reliable....professional....

PROFESSIONAL HIGHLIGHTS

Valley Memorial Hospital   1993 to Present
Pleasanton, California
Registered Nurse

Position responsibilities include the following:

- Patient assessment, medication, P.O., I.M., and I.V., and total patient care.
- Care and monitoring of laboring patients including fetal monitoring, pitocin and
  prostin induction, and care of postpartum patients.

Accomplishments: Commended by management for the quality and consistency of my
performance.

Dominican Hospital   1988 -1993
Santa Cruz, California
Registered Nurse

- Instructing patients in diabetic care, skin and wound care, nutrition, exercise, and
  total patient care.
- Cardiac rehabilitation, monitoring telemetry, and preparing patients for various
  procedures.
- Worked in med / surg, neuro / respiratory, oncology, CCU / ICU, and telemetry units.
- Primary and team leading nursing.

EDUCATION

ADN Degree, Chabot College, Graduated with HONORS

STRENGTHS

Solid background of effective nursing, with patience, care and a genuine desire to help people.

REFERENCES EXCELLENT AND AVAILABLE UPON REQUEST

JACK W. WRIGHT
2773 Carmen Avenue
Livermore, California 94550
Telephone: 510 443 4327

OFFICE MANAGER

Available to discuss a challenging and responsible position
where my education and experience can be fully
utilized to our mutual benefit.

Summary of Skills

....formal education....experienced in office management....customer relations and service....staff supervision and training....office machines.....typing.....data entry...... planning and scheduling.... computerized operations......developing work flow systems ....planning and scheduling....record keeping working with vendors....reports.....heavy phone interface......accounting.....excellent communication skills......pride in quality performance and achievement....ability to work well with all levels of management and personnel....reliable....professional....

PROFESSIONAL HIGHLIGHTS

Poretics Corporation   1990 to Present
Pleasanton, California
Office Manager
Position responsibilities include administering all office functions including development of work flow systems, supervision, accounting, and customer service.
Duties include: the following:
- Conducting customer transactions in a friendly, courteous and expedient manner.
- Maintaining files of customer records from installations, including services rendered.
- Effectively prioritizing and organizing work loads in a constantly changing environment to meet daily and weekly schedules.

Accomplishments: Commended by management for the quality and consistency of my performance. 1992 Employee of the Year Award.

Community Television / CTV 30   1983 - 1990
Danville, California
Freelance Work
Responsible for working in all areas of studio / field television production. Primary Camera / studio hand.

EDUCATION

AA Degree in Arts and Sciences, Richland College,
Dallas, Texas.

STRENGTHS

Ability to create and present an excellent image of the company and its services to customers, and to coordinate and communicate well with clientele and management at all levels and efficiently meet objectives.

REFERENCES EXCELLENT AND AVAILABLE UPON REQUEST

JACK W. WRIGHT
2773 Carmen Avenue
Livermore, California 94550
Telephone: 510 443 4327

PARAMEDIC

Available to discuss a challenging and responsible position
where my education and experience can be fully
utilized to our mutual benefit.

Summary of Skills

....formal education....ambulance driver's permit......experienced in life support systems ....cardiac care.....intensive care.....psychiatric care.....burns.....patient and people handling skills......policies and procedures......ability to work under pressure......office management......customer relations and service......staff supervision and training...... computerized operations....record keeping.....reports...excellent communication skills.... pride in quality performance and achievement....ability to work well with all levels of management and personnel....reliable....professional....

EDUCATION

Completed 9 month Program of Paramedic education at the Center for Pre-hospital Research & Training, University of California, San Francisco.
Coursework included:
* 384 hours of Didactic Work that exceeds D.O.T. Guidelines.
* 240 hours of clinical Work at various San Francisco Hospitals.
* 480 hours of Field Internship with the San Francisco Department of Public Health, Paramedic Division.

The 240 hours of hospital experience at S.F. General included: Live Intubations, Psychiatric Emergency Services, Intensive care, Cardiac Care, and Mobile Intensive Care Base Station.
Clinical Experience includes the Burn Center at Saint Francis, and the UCSF Emergency Department.

While Pursuing Education

Mercy Life Care, Inc.   3 / 93 to Present
Pleasanton, California
Emergency Medical Technician
Position responsibilities include:
* Routine interfacility transfers, emergency and non-emergency transportation of patients.
* Emergency pre-hospital stabilization of patients prior to transport.
* Interagency networking in providing pre-hospital care for patients.

CERTIFICATES
Pediatric Advanced Life Support (PALS) Certificate.
Basic Trauma Life Support (BTLS) Certificate.
Dallas, Texas.

REFERENCES EXCELLENT AND AVAILABLE UPON REQUEST

JACK W. WRIGHT
2773 Carmen Avenue
Livermore, California 94550
Telephone: 510 443 4327

PHARMACY TECHNICIAN

Available to discuss a challenging and responsible position
where my education and experience can be fully
utilized to our mutual benefit.

Summary of Skills

.....formal education.....experienced with basic calculations....drug nomenclature.... basic pharmacology...drug distribution systems....basic compound and IV admixture ....insurance billings....Medicare....medical prescription requirements....controlled substances....computerized operations...inventory control....cash flow management ....customer relations and service...working with vendors...excellent communication skills....pride in quality performance and achievement....ability to work well with all levels of management and personnel....reliable....professional....

EDUCATION

Presently pursuing externship to apply skills and complete Western career College's Certificate Program for Pharmacy Technician. Course includes:

- Pharmacy law and ethics, telephone techniques, and clerical procedures.
- Pharmacy reference books, pharmacology and physiology, and drug distribution.
- Prescriptions, chemistry, and controlled substances.
- Equipment, computer training, and over-the-counter products.
- Organizing, replenishing and maintaining a comprehensive product knowledge.
- Knowledge of pharmaceutical terminology utilized to contact physicians for refill authorizations.
- Reconstituting and preparing IV admixtures and syringes, prepackaging various bulk medications, and admixing TPN's.

While Pursuing Education

Long Drugs   3/ 93 to Present
Pleasanton, California
Sales Clerk
Responsible for sales counter and assisting customer with product selection.

STRENGTHS

Ability to create and present an excellent image of the company and its services to customers, and to coordinate and communicate well with clientele and management at all levels and efficiently meet objectives.

REFERENCES EXCELLENT AND AVAILABLE UPON REQUEST

JACK W. WRIGHT
2773 Carmen Avenue
Livermore, California 94550
Telephone: 510 443 4327

PHLEBOTOMIST / MEDICAL ASSISTANT

Available to discuss a challenging and responsible entry level
position where my education and experience can be
fully utilized to our mutual benefit.

Summary of Skills

....formal education....experienced in phlebotomy...patient relations and service....medical terminology....office procedures....medical accounting....laboratory techniques......pharmacology......clinical procedures......EKG's......CPR certification......phlebotomy certified......medical assistant certification......excellent communication skills....pride in quality performance and achievement......ability to work well with all levels of management and personnel....reliable....professional....

PROFESSIONAL HIGHLIGHTS

VA Hospital   11/ 93 - 1/ 94
Livermore, California
Phlebotomist

Position responsibilities include the following volunteer work:

- Preparing patients for examination according to protocol, and maintaining and documenting patient charts.
- Basic laboratory screenings and venipunctures, cleaning, and maintaining inventory.
- Effectively prioritizing and organizing work loads in a constantly changing environment to meet daily and weekly deadlines.

Dr. Jerry Yen   1992 -1993
Pleasanton, California
Back Office Assistant
Responsibilities included preparing patients, taking vital signs, interviewing patients, drawing blood, and maintaining charts and records.

EDUCATION

Completed Classes in General Education,
Las Positas Community College, Livermore, California
Graduated from Med-Help Training School, Concord, California,
and completed 4 week Externship at Muir Medical Center.

STRENGTHS

Ability to quickly establish a positive and productive rapport with patients marked by care and a genuine desire to help people.

REFERENCES EXCELLENT AND AVAILABLE UPON REQUEST

JACK W. WRIGHT
2773 Carmen Avenue
Livermore, California 94550
Telephone: 510 443 4327

POLICE OFFICER

Available to discuss a challenging and responsible entry level
position where my education and experience can be
fully utilized to our mutual benefit.

Summary of Skills

....formal education....experienced in retail security....investigations....field tactics ....surveillance....stakeouts....tear gas....batons....first aid....CPR....public relations and service....staff supervision and training....creative problem solving... planning and scheduling.....reports.....ability to work well with all levels of management and personnel......pride in quality performance and achievement.......reliable....... competent....

EDUCATION

Chabot College, Completed PC 832 Module A, Commission of Peace Officer Standards and Training in Powers of Arrest and Firearms Familiarization and Safety.
Martinez Adult School, Completed PC 832 Module B, Peace Officers Standard of Training Reserve Officer Level II.
Martinez Adult School, PC 832 Module C, Peace Officers Standard and Training Reserve Officer Level I.

ADDITIONAL

Permit for Exposed Firearms includes the .38, .357, 9mm and .45
Registered State of California Security Guard
State of California Baton Permit - Tear Gas Certificate
Certificate for Standard First Aid (new method) and CPR
Certificate for the use of Chemical Agents
Certified in Defense Tactics & High Risk Field Tactics

WORK EXPERIENCE

Pelican Security Training Agency, Pleasanton, CA (1990 - 1991)
Interstate security, Fremont, CA (2/ 90 to 4/ 92)
Guardian Security, Concord, CA (2/ 93 to Present)
University of the Pacific, Stockton, CA (8/ 93 - Present)
Duties included stakeouts, security, investigations, and surveillance.

STRENGTHS

High professional level, excellence of leadership technique, and professional attention to detail supplemented by the ability to influence and stimulate others.

REFERENCES EXCELLENT AND AVAILABLE UPON REQUEST

109

JACK W. WRIGHT
2773 Carmen Avenue
Livermore, California 94550
Telephone: 510 443 4327
PRESS OPERATOR
Available to discuss a challenging and responsible entry level
position where my education and experience can be
fully utilized to our mutual benefit.

Summary of Skills

....over 8 years experience in all phases of printing...experienced in offset....multicolor ....registration....mixing and running PMS colors....Benday....half tones....pasteup.... bindery......stripping......press troubleshooting and maintenance....T-head......creative problem solver....excellent communication skills....ability to work well with all levels of management and personnel....pride in quality performance and achievement....reliable ....professional....

PROFESSIONAL HIGHLIGHTS

Standard Register   3/ 90 to Present
Pleasanton, California
Lithographer
Position responsibilities include high quality, multi - color printing for commercial trade. Duties include the following:
· Operation, troubleshooting and maintenance of A.B. Dick 9800 series offset duplicator.
· Daily operation, setup and cleaning of press.
· Effectively prioritizing and organizing work loads in a constantly changing environment to meet daily and weekly deadlines.
· Selecting and working with a wide variety of paper stock, sizes and weights.
Accomplishments: Was commended for exceeding the daily production quota of 30,000 impressions per day by 67,000.

Excel Graphics   1987 - 1990
San Ramon, California
Press Operator
Responsibilities included operation and maintenance of offset printing equipment for this privately owned print shop. Worked with a wide variety of paper stocks, sizes and weights.

STRENGTHS

Career reflects hard work, attention to detail, and the ability to meet exact specifications as well as cost, quality, safety and time objectives.

REFERENCES EXCELLENT AND AVAILABLE UPON REQUEST

JACK W. WRIGHT
2773 Carmen Avenue
Livermore, California 94550
Telephone: 510 443 4327
PRODUCTION CONTROL
Available to discuss a challenging and responsible entry level
position where my education and experience can be
fully utilized to our mutual benefit.

Summary of Skills

......formal training......experienced in all areas of production control......staff supervision and training......coordinating production schedule to customer demand....scheduling staff....developing work flow systems....analyzing.... problem solving....computerized systems....cost estimations....record keeping .....reports.....quality control.....statistics......excellent communication skills..... ability to work well with all levels of management and personnel.....pride in quality performance and achievement....reliable....professional....

PROFESSIONAL HIGHLIGHTS

The Last Factory   1985 to Present
Livermore, California
Production Manager
Position responsibilities include supervision of shipping & receiving, purchasing of all raw materials, inventory control, material handling, budgeting, and working with vendors. Specific duties include:
- Preparing sales trends on monthly, quarterly, and annual basis for presentation to the Marketing Division.
- Reviewing sales trends and adjusting the stock levels to account for product expiration dates.
- Preparing and making presentations to management regarding the status of various products, anticipated demands, or problems with the department.
- Reviewing movement of stock at all points of distribution in stores and recommending appropriate disposition in cases of shortages or overstocks.

Accomplishments: Established new inventory control, warehouse, and order pulling systems. Also researched and found the most cost effective suppliers which resulted in a net savings of over 40% annually.

J.C. Paper Company   1981 - 1985
Oakland, California
Store Manager

STRENGTHS

Career reflecting total involvement, high motivation, persuasive interaction and communication with people, eagerness to work, and proven leadership qualities.

REFERENCES EXCELLENT AND AVAILABLE UPON REQUEST

111

JACK W. WRIGHT
2773 Carmen Avenue
Livermore, California 94550
Telephone: 510 443 4327

PROPERTY MANAGEMENT

Available to discuss a challenging and responsible entry level
position where my education and experience can be
fully utilized to our mutual benefit.

Summary of Skills

....over 6 years experience in managing property....experienced in customer relations and service....staff supervision and training.....applicant screening...... advertising....personnel management......collections.....coordinating maintenance ....working with subcontractors......marketing....office....reports administration.... credit checks...evictions....record keeping.....ability to work well with all levels of management and personnel.....pride in quality performance and achievement.... reliable....professional....

PROFESSIONAL HIGHLIGHTS

BLD Investments   1992 to Present
Livermore, California
On-Site Property Manager
Position responsibilities include managing and maintaining complex for maximum occupancy. Duties include:
- Renting, collecting rent monies, banking, remodeling, screening tenants, and credit checks.
- Rent control inspections, supervision of subcontractors, and eviction and court procedures.

Accomplishments: Increased occupancy from 42% to 100%.

San Leandro Racquet Club   1988 - 1992
San Leandro, California
Assistant Manager / Leasing Agent
Renting apartments, qualifying applicants, handling all telephone and walk-in traffic, moving in new tenants, and processing all service requests. Also assisted in preparing legal matters for attorneys.

STRENGTHS

Dedicated professional offering versatility and enthusiasm with an aptitude for developing effective, efficient programs and converting new ideas into profitable results.

REFERENCES EXCELLENT AND AVAILABLE UPON REQUEST

JACK W. WRIGHT

2773 Carmen Avenue
Livermore, California 94550
Telephone: 510 443 4327

QUALITY CONTROL

Available to discuss a challenging and responsible entry level
position where my education and experience can be
fully utilized to our mutual benefit.

Summary of Skills

....formal training...experienced in quality assurance.....production.....PC assembly ....manufacturing....cable harnesses.....documentation......sampling......inventory control....hardware and software....soldering....wire wrap....PC board rework..... component identification....color codes...reports...diagrams....schematics ....parts lists......parts placement......assembly diagrams......familiar with all standard test equipment.....excellent communication skills.....ability to work well with all levels of management and personnel.....pride in quality performance and achievement ....reliable....professional....

PROFESSIONAL HIGHLIGHTS

Magnetic Pulse, Inc.   1989 to Present
Fremont, California
Electrical Inspector
Position responsibilities include:
- Progress inspection of PWA's, cables, and electrical connections.
- Inspecting cable routing in chassis assemblies and reporting field discrepancies and failures.
- Inspection of electrical components and final inspection of assemblies, systems and pressure seals.

Accomplishments: Was awarded Certificate of Excellence for my performance.

General Electric - CALMA   1984 - 1989
Milipitas, California
Administration Specialist
Duties included maintaining HP3000 database, utilizing Cognos EXPERT to provide customized reports, creating hardware and software configurations for new customers, and QA inspection of software update shipments.

STRENGTHS

Career reflects hard work, attention to detail, and the ability to meet exact specifications as well as cost, quality, safety and time objectives.

REFERENCES EXCELLENT AND AVAILABLE UPON REQUEST

JACK W. WRIGHT

2773 Carmen Avenue
Livermore, California 94550
Telephone: 510 443 4327

REAL ESTATE / NEW HOME SALES

Available to discuss a challenging and responsible position
where my education and experience can be fully
utilized to our mutual benefit.

Summary of Skills

....formal education....over 13 years experience in real estate sales and marketing.... experienced in customer relations and service...sales presentations....sales plans and procedures..... staff supervision and training....California real estate license.... financing packages....escrow follow-up....persuasive presentation and closing skills ....contracts....excellent communication skills....pride in quality performance and achievement....ability to work well with all levels of management and personnel ....reliable....professional....

PROFESSIONAL HIGHLIGHTS

Wellbilt Homes   1990 to Present
Dublin, California
Sales Counselor
Responsible for setting up the sales office and assisted in all aspects for this move up market of single family homes. Duties included:
- Prequalifying buyers for financing, counseling on various financing packages, and assisted with lot and floorplan selection.
- Negotiated Deposit Receipts with management, opened escrows, ordered options, and followed through with all applicable paperwork through close of escrow.
- Worked with construction superintendents, upper management, appraisers, architects, and decorators.

Accomplishments: Consistently earned outstanding performance awards - 9 Million Producer.

Coldwell Banker   1984 - 1990
Byron, California
Sales Associate / Manager

EDUCATION
Diablo Valley College
Anthony School of Real Estate - Coldwell Banker Management Training

STRENGTHS
Ability to create and present an excellent image of the company and its services to customers, and to coordinate and communicate well with clientele and management at all levels and efficiently meet objectives.

REFERENCES EXCELLENT AND AVAILABLE UPON REQUEST

JACK W. WRIGHT
2773 Carmen Avenue
Livermore, California 94550
Telephone: 510 443 4327

RECEPTIONIST/ OFFICE MANAGEMENT

Available to discuss a challenging and responsible position
where my education and experience can be fully
utilized to our mutual benefit.

Summary of Skills

....formal education.....experienced in office management.....customer relations and service...accounts payable and receivable...bookkeeping and accounting....assessing customer needs....credit and collections....filing....payroll....computerized systems.... office machines.....record keeping.....reports.....staff supervision and training....... excellent communication skills......pride in quality performance and achievement..... ability to work well with all levels of management and personnel......reliable...... professional....

PROFESSIONAL HIGHLIGHTS

Dr. McCallum   1980 - 1993
Livermore, California
Front Office

Position responsibilities include the following:

· Performing work with minimal direction and establishing priorities independently on a daily basis.
· Conducting customer transactions in a friendly, courteous, and expedient manner.
· Answering phones, screening correspondence, and typing memos and documents.
· Effectively prioritizing and organizing work loads in a constantly changing environment to meet daily and weekly deadlines.
· Preparing patients for examination according to protocol, and maintaining and documenting patient charts.
· Filling out insurance forms and related paperwork for insurance billings.
Accomplishments: Commended on numerous occasions for the quality and consistency of my performance.

Dr. Robert Wildrick   1975 - 1980
Castro Valley, California
Office Manager / Chairside Assistant

EDUCATION
Graduated from Oakland College for Dental / Medical Assistants

STRENGTHS

Ability to create and present an excellent image of the company and its services to customers, and to coordinate and communicate well with clientele and management at all levels and efficiently meet objectives.

REFERENCES EXCELLENT AND AVAILABLE UPON REQUEST

JACK W. WRIGHT
2773 Carmen Avenue
Livermore, California 94550
Telephone: 510 443 4327

SALES REPRESENTATIVE

Available to discuss a challenging and responsible position
where my education and experience can be fully
utilized to our mutual benefit.

Summary of Skills

.....formal education....experienced in sales and marketing....customer relations and service......securing new accounts by appointments and cold calling...... promotionals....plans and procedures....creating displays....sales presentations..... pricing.....sales plans and procedures.....customer quotes.....staff supervision and training.....excellent communication skills......pride in quality performance and achievement....ability to work well with all levels of management and personnel ....reliable....professional....

PROFESSIONAL HIGHLIGHTS

Acme Sales, Inc.   1992 to Present
San Jose, California
Sales Representative

Position responsibilities include the following:

- Relating merchandise statistics to use of floor space to maximize sales and profit.
- Creating floor arrangements, displays, and working with clients in product selection.
- Insuring orders are filled in a timely manner and immediately notifying customers of any delays.
- Facilitating customer awareness through individual sales presentations and productive sales meetings.
- Conducting customer transactions in a friendly, courteous, and expedient manner.
- Making sales calls on current and potential customers and initiating product orders.

Ajax Sales   1991 -1992
Hayward, California
Salesman

Duties included merchandising, retail sales, customer service, inventory control, and training new employees in company sales procedures.

EDUCATION

AA Degree in General Education, Las Positas Community College. *
* Will graduate in 1996

STRENGTHS

Ability to create and present an excellent image of the company and its services to customers, and to coordinate and communicate well with clientele and management at all levels and efficiently meet objectives.

REFERENCES EXCELLENT AND AVAILABLE UPON REQUEST

SHIRLEY A. WRIGHT

2773 Carmen Avenue
Livermore, California 94550
Telephone: 510 443 4327

SECRETARY / OFFICE MANAGER

Available to discuss a challenging and responsible position
where my education and experience can be fully
utilized to our mutual benefit.

Summary of Skills

....formal education....experienced in customer relations and service....staff supervision and training....data entry....maintaining patients records and charts....heavy phones... medical terminology....insurance and consent forms....billings....office procedures..... excellent communication skills.....pride in quality performance and achievement...... ability to work well with all levels of management and personnel......competent...... professional....

PROFESSIONAL HIGHLIGHTS

Fu Man chu M. D.   1992 - 1994
Castro Valley, California
Receptionist
Was in complete charge of the front office and responsible for phones, filing, scheduling, data entry, billing, medical records, and new patient charts and information.

Dr. Louis Nelson   1988 - 1992
Fresno, California
Office Manager
Duties much the same as above and included light dictation.

Cummings Trucking   1988 - 1991
Fresno, California
Dispatcher

Stanislaus County Hospital   1984 - 1988
Modesto, California
Ward Clerk

EDUCATION

Diploma as Medical Receptionist, Mid-State Medical College, Modesto, California.
Completed Classes in Business Administration, Modesto Junior College.
Medicare Insurance Classes and Dun & Bradstreet Collection Classes.

STRENGTHS

Ability to create and present an excellent image of the company and its services to customers, and to coordinate and communicate well with clientele and management at all levels and efficiently meet objectives.

REFERENCES EXCELLENT AND AVAILABLE UPON REQUEST

JACK W. WRIGHT
2773 Carmen Avenue
Livermore, California 94550
Telephone: 510 443 4327

SECURITY / INVESTIGATIONS

Available to discuss a challenging and responsible position
where my education and experience can be fully
utilized to our mutual benefit.

Summary of Skills

....formal education....over 15 years experience....experienced in all phases of law enforcement......supervision.....investigations.....fingerprint expert......cited for bravery....fraud....burglary....theft....crimonology....client relations and service.... stake-outs.....reports.....excellent communication skills.......pride in quality performance and achievement....ability to work well with all levels of management and personnel.... competent....professional....

PROFESSIONAL HIGHLIGHTS

Alameda County Sheriff's Department   1989 - 1994
Oakland, California
Deputy Sheriff
Law enforcement in rural and urban areas. Investigated accidents, burglary, theft, malicious mischief, minor fraud, etc. Fingerprint expert with administrative responsibilities for 8 to 12 personnel in the department. Also worked as a bailiff and jailer.
Accomplishments: Cited for bravery by V.F.W.

State of California   1985 - 1989
Compton, California
Parole Officer
Responsibilities included supervision of inmates recently released from state prison and pre-release investigations.

EDUCATION
BA Degree in Liberal Arts, San Francisco State College.
AA Degree in Criminology, San Francisco City College.
Completed Classes in Management, Chabot College.

STRENGTHS

High professional level, excellence of leadership technique, and professional attention to detail supplemented by the ability to influence and stimulate others.

REFERENCES EXCELLENT AND AVAILABLE UPON REQUEST

JACK W. WRIGHT
2773 Carmen Avenue
Livermore, California 94550
Telephone: 510 443 4327

SHIPPING AND RECEIVING

Available to discuss a challenging and responsible position
where my education and experience can be fully
utilized to our mutual benefit.

Summary of Skills

.....formal education....experienced in all areas of shipping and receiving....staff supervision and training....material handling....maintaining stock levels ....storage and issuing parts....inventory control....warehouse operations.... UPS and freight bill paperwork......documentation.....reports.....excellent communication skills.... career desire....pride in quality performance and achievement...... ability to work well with all levels of management and personnel....competent....professional....

PROFESSIONAL HIGHLIGHTS

Service Manufacturing   1989 to Present
Oakland, California
Shipping/ Receiving Supervisor
Responsibilities include:
- Supervision of employees and loading and unloading of trucks.
- UPS and freight bill paperwork, and inventory control.
- Customer relations and service, detail shop controller, and fork lift operation.

Accomplishments: Reorganized department for more productive operation, including providing faster service with less returns.

Professional Glass Products   1985 - 1989
Livermore, California
Shipping / Receiving Clerk
Responsibilities included pulling and shipping of scientific glass products, operating a fork lift and acting as warehouse controller.

EDUCATION
1 year of Business Classes, Northern Virginia Community College.

STRENGTHS
Ability to create and present an excellent image of the company and its services to customers, and to coordinate and communicate well with clientele and management at all levels and efficiently meet objectives.

REFERENCES EXCELLENT AND AVAILABLE UPON REQUEST

119

JACK W. WRIGHT

2773 Carmen Avenue
Livermore, California 94550
Telephone: 510 443 4327

SYSTEMS ANALYST

Available to discuss a challenging and responsible position
where my education and experience can be fully
utilized to our mutual benefit.

Summary of Skills

.....formal education......languages include COBOL, MVS - REXX, BASIC, Foxbase, PASCAL, ALGOL, FORTRAN, and PC Assembler......operating systems include MVS / XA-ESA, DOS / VSE, VM, MSDOS, RTE - PLUS, and MCP....environmental software includes CICS, SDF, DB2, VSAM, ADR / DATACOM DB ISPF, MVS - JCL, FILE - AID, IDCAMS, PROEDIT, SPUFI, QMF, XPEDITER, INTERTEST, SMARTTEST, and NOVELL / NETWARE.....LANS......hardware includes IBM-3090, IBM-4361, IBM PCs, HP-1000, and Burroughs 1900 & 6800......experienced in planning and analysis......design and development....testing and debugging....documentation.....staff supervision and training......excellent communication skills......pride in quality performance and achievement....ability to work well with all levels of management and personnel....reliable....professional....

PROFESSIONAL HIGHLIGHTS

AT&T   1989 to Present
Dublin, California
Systems Analyst
Position accomplishments include seeing projects through from initial concept and design to the final debugging and production. Accomplishments include:
- Design, development, and testing of billing application systems on an IBM-3090 under MVS using COBOL II, DB2, FILE AID etc.
- Developed and tested Format InfraStructure modules for the Billing Project.
- Designed, developed and tested the Stack & Burst Paper and Fiche modules.
- Written REXX routines including a generic MENU structure in REXX using DB2 & DMS.

The Computer Company   1990 - 1991
Glen Allen, Virginia
Systems Analyst
Duties included development, conversion (ASSEMBLER to COBOL) and testing of Online and Batch Programs for the New Mexico Medicaid System on the IBM-3090 under MVS using CICS, COBOL, JCL, FILE-AID, etc..

EDUCATION

B.E (Hons.) - Mechanical and M.Sc (Hons.) - Mathematics from UCLA.

REFERENCES EXCELLENT AND AVAILABLE UPON REQUEST

JACK W. WRIGHT
2773 Carmen Avenue
Livermore, California 94550
Telephone: 510 443 4327

ELEMENTARY TEACHER

Available to discuss a challenging and responsible position
where my education and experience can be fully
utilized to our mutual benefit.

Summary of Skills

.....formal education.....early childhood education....California State Teaching Credential....experienced in writing curriculum....testing....computer literate ....parent conferences.....multi - cultural students.....special needs students..... recording students progress.....planning individual and group activities...... excellent communication skills......ability to interface well with parents and other teachers.....competent.....professional....

PROFESSIONAL HIGHLIGHTS

Livermore Valley Unified Schools   1986 to Present
Livermore, California
Substitute Teacher
Responsible for teaching many subjects with very little notice. Duties include:
- Teaching various subjects, often in difficult situations where adequate planning by regular teacher was not possible.
- Curriculum development, budgeting, and teaching a variety of socially and physically handicapped children.
Accomplishments: Commended for my performance and was awarded "Humanitarian Award" from local TV station.

Livermore Valley Unified Schools   1984 - 1986
Livermore, California
Special Education Teacher
Responsible for helping students with a variety of social and physical handicaps to learn basic life skills. This included curriculum development, budgeting, teaching, and working with and counseling parents.

EDUCATION
BA Degree in Early Childhood Education, California State Polytechnic,
San Louis Obisbo, California.

STRENGTHS

Expertise in diagnosis, design, and implementation of individualized remedial and educational strategies with patience, care, and a genuine desire to help people.

REFERENCES EXCELLENT AND AVAILABLE UPON REQUEST

JACK W. WRIGHT
2773 Carmen Avenue
Livermore, California 94550
Telephone: 510 443 4327

TRAFFIC MANAGER / TRANSPORTATION
Available to discuss a challenging and responsible position
where my education and experience can be fully
utilized to our mutual benefit.

Summary of Skills

......formal education......experienced in all areas of transportation......rate quotations.....auditing.....account billing.....negotiations.....contracts.....client relations and service.....tarrifs.....exports.....tracing.....updating records and vendors......computerized operations......staff supervision and training...... material handling requirements.....planning and scheduling.....ability to work under pressure....billings....excellent communication skills......ability to work well with all levels of management and personnel....competent...reliable.... professional...

PROFESSIONAL HIGHLIGHTS

Oakland Traffic Service   1986 to Present
Oakland, California
Assistant Traffic Manager
Responsible for researching and coordinating piggyback moves. Duties include:
- Billing of trailers and containers with the various railroads.
- Tracing trailers and making inquiries into problem trailers as necessary.
- Dispatching draymen and taking their releases.
- Rate quotations and updating truck, rail and customer records.
- Researching accounts payable for discrepancies, and supervision of office staff.

Delta Lines, Inc.   1984 - 1986
Oakland, California
Rate Auditor
Duties included rate quotations, accounts payable interline adjustments, and assuring the accuracy and application of appropriate rates.
Accomplishments: Was instrumental in a significant cost savings by discontinuing unprofitable interlines.

EDUCATION
AA Degree in Distribution and Traffic Management, Chabot College,
Hayward, California.

STRENGTHS
Career reflects hard work, attention to detail, and the ability to meet exact specifications as well as cost, quality, safety and time objectives.

REFERENCES EXCELLENT AND AVAILABLE UPON REQUEST

JACK W. WRIGHT

2773 Carmen Avenue
Livermore, California 94550
Telephone: 510 443 4327

TRAINING

Available to discuss a challenging and responsible position
where my education and experience can be fully
utilized to our mutual benefit.

Summary of Skills

...formal education....experienced in designing and developing training programs ....platform presentations....customer relations and service...project management .... word processing....computerized operations....contracts.... staff supervision and training....proposals....testing....planning and scheduling....problem solving ....excellent organizational and communication skills......ability to work well with all levels of management and personnel.... competent...reliable....professional...

PROFESSIONAL HIGHLIGHTS

Pacific Bell   1984 to Present
San Ramon, California
Technical Trainer (1990 to Present)
Responsibilities include job analysis, data collection, course design and development, course instruction, follow-up evaluation and:
- All phases of course development for marketing and orderwriter training.
- Maintaining project files, and meetings and interface with Methods, Tariffs, and product teams regarding changes that affect training.
- Close liaison with Product Management and Methods to develop new courses targeted for Business Service Representatives statewide.
- Working with budgets and proposals for funding and course tuition.

Pac Bell
Orange, California
Training Instructor (1984 - 1990)

EDUCATION

Technical training in all phases of Project Manager Course Development and Instruction Skills. Courses included instruction of self-paced and leader-led material.

STRENGTHS

Career reflects hard work, attention to detail, and the ability to meet exact specifications as well as cost, quality, safety and time objectives.

REFERENCES EXCELLENT AND AVAILABLE UPON REQUEST

JACK W. WRIGHT
2773 Carmen Avenue
Livermore, California 94550
Telephone: 510 443 4327

TRAVEL CONSULTANT

Available to discuss a challenging and responsible position
where my education and experience can be fully
utilized to our mutual benefit.

Summary of Skills

......formal training......experienced in all areas of travel......computerized operations....customer relations and service....travel counseling....selling and arranging group travel.....airline and travel documentation.....international travel.....tours.....complex itineraries.....regulations....restrictions.....reports..... excellent organizational and communication skills......ability to work well with all levels of management and personnel....competent....professional....

PROFESSIONAL HIGHLIGHTS

Biscayne Travel Corporation   1992 to Present
Miami, Florida
Travel Consultant
Responsibilities include working with clients in selecting and planning travel itineraries and arrangements. Duties include:

- Insuring customer satisfaction by investigating and resolving customer problems relating to policy and pricing.
- Effectively prioritizing and organizing travel plans in a constantly changing environment to meet daily and weekly schedules.
- Surveys to determine the lowest travel cost consistent with quality, reliability, and the ability to meet required schedules.

EDUCATION

Graduated from Echols International Training Course, San Francisco, California.

Coursework included:

- Travel Agency Operations, Geography and Tourist Locations, and Cruises.
- Domestic and International Land Tours, and Domestic and International Rail principles.
- Group Travel, Airline and Travel Documentation, and Hotel and Rental Cars.
- ARC Industry Agent's Handbook, Basic and Advanced Computer training and Marketing and Sales Techniques.

STRENGTHS

Ability to create and present an excellent image of the company and its services to customers, and to coordinate and communicate well with clientele and management at all levels and efficiently meet objectives.

REFERENCES EXCELLENT AND AVAILABLE UPON REQUEST

JACK W. WRIGHT
2773 Carmen Avenue
Livermore, California 94550
Telephone: 510 443 4327
TRUCK DRIVER
Available to discuss a challenging and responsible position
where my education and experience can be fully
utilized to our mutual benefit.

Summary of Skills

....formal training....over 15 years experience....possess a valid commercial class "A" license....current medical certificate....experienced with on-board CADEC computer...paperwork...precheck inspections...safety...government requirements ....customer relations and service....truck maintenance....reefers....basic food handling....pre-trip inspections....driving rules and inspections....logs....material handling....ability to work well with all levels of management and personnel.... competent....professional....

PROFESSIONAL HIGHLIGHTS

Foodmaker Distribution, Inc.   1980 to Present
Hayward, California
Truck Driver
Responsible for making deliveries and pickups to all restaurants on assigned route. Duties include:

- Using the CADEC on-board computer to enter destinations and delivery times using proper codes.
- Performing standard D O T precheck and company inspections prior to beginning all trips.
- Paperwork and invoices, including add-on, hot shots, backhauls, and additions and deletions.
- Inspecting pallets and re-stacking between deliveries to prevent damage to other products in the trailer.

Accomplishments: Commended by management for the consistency and quality of my performance. Received company's Safe Driving Award for every year of service.

ADDITIONAL
Completed Company Sponsored Safe Driving program - Excellent DMV Record.

STRENGTHS
Career reflects hard work, attention to detail, and the ability to meet exact specifications as well as cost, quality, safety and time objectives.

REFERENCES EXCELLENT AND AVAILABLE UPON REQUEST

JACK W. WRIGHT
2773 Carmen Avenue
Livermore, California 94550
Telephone: 510 443 4327

VETERINARY ASSISTANT / RECEPTIONIST
Available to discuss a challenging and responsible position
where my education and experience can be fully
utilized to our mutual benefit.

Summary of Skills

......formal education......experienced in customer relations and service.......office management....office machines....filing....10-Key by touch....typing....computerized operations....heavy phone interface....record keeping....reports.....developing work flow systems.....planning and scheduling.....good organizational skills......excellent communication skills......ability to work under pressure......career desire......love of animals....ability to work well with all levels of management and personnel....pride in quality performance and achievement....reliable....professional....

PROFESSIONAL HIGHLIGHTS

Department of the Air Force   1985 to Present
NAS Moffett Field, California
Production Controller

Position responsibilities include the following:

- Answering phones, screening correspondence, and typing memos and documents.
- Performing work independently with minimal direction and establishing priorities independently on a daily basis.
- Effectively organizing work loads in a constantly changing environment to meet daily and weekly deadlines.
- Conducting customer transactions in a friendly, courteous and expedient manner.

Accomplishments: Commended by management on numerous occasions for the quality and consistency of my performance.

Tri - Valley Animal Rescue   1992 to Present
Livermore, California
Volunteer
Duties included the fostering, care and placement of abandoned animals.

EDUCATION
AA Degree in General Education, Las Positas Community College. *
* Will graduate in 1996.

STRENGTHS
Ability to create and present an excellent image of the company and its services to customers, and to coordinate and communicate well with clientele and management at all levels and efficiently meet objectives.

REFERENCES EXCELLENT AND AVAILABLE UPON REQUEST

SHIRLEY A. WRIGHT
2773 Carmen Avenue
Livermore, California 94550
Telephone: 510 443 4327

WAITRESS

Available to discuss a challenging and responsible position
where my education and experience can be fully
utilized to our mutual benefit.

Summary of Skills

.....over 6 years experience in food service and preparation......customer relations and service....scheduling staff....opening and closing....training employees....food serving.... tray service....inventory....cash management....food industry career desire....paperwork ....closing out cash receipts....people handling skills....ability to work under pressure.... ability to work well with all levels of management and personnel....pride in quality performance and achievement....reliable....professional....

PROFESSIONAL HIGHLIGHTS

Kountry Kitchen   1992 to Present
Pleasanton, California
Waitress
Position responsibilities include insuring prompt delivery of food, resolving customer problems, closing out cash receipts, handling paperwork involved, etc. Accomplishments: Commended by management on numerous occasions for the quality and consistency of my performance.

JR's   1985 - 1992
Livermore, California
Waitress / Food Preparation
Duties included the fostering, care and placement of abandoned animals.

Denny's   1984 - 1985
Redwood City, California
Waitress

EDUCATION
Completed Classes in General Education,
Las Positas Community College, Livermore, California

STRENGTHS

Enthusiastic and positive, able to create and present a top flight image of the restaurant and its service to customers and to bring a personal yet effective touch to the job.

REFERENCES EXCELLENT AND AVAILABLE UPON REQUEST

JACK W. WRIGHT
2773 Carmen Avenue
Livermore, California 94550
Telephone: 510 443 4327

WAREHOUSEMAN

Available to discuss a challenging and responsible position
where my education and experience can be fully
utilized to our mutual benefit.

Summary of Skills

......formal education......experienced in all areas of warehousing......shipping and receiving.....inventory control....material handling....computerized systems....record keeping.....maintaining stock levels.....billings......reports.....data entry...customer relations and service......cash flow management......problem solving......ability to work under pressure......excellent communication skills......ability to work well with all levels of management and personnel....pride in quality performance and achievement.... reliable....

PROFESSIONAL HIGHLIGHTS

The Harper Group   1992 - 1993
San Francisco, California
Facilities Manager

Position responsibilities include the following:

- Controlling inventory, stocking, ordering from vendors, and inspection of materials.
- UPS and freight bill paperwork, loading and unloading of trucks, forklift operation, and storage management.
- Reviewing sales trends and adjusting stock levels to account for product expiration dates.
- Monitoring inventory levels and stock status of assigned products.
- Maintaining a minimum stock level while insuring store and customers receive proper service.
- Verifying a wide variety of material against receiving documents, and reporting discrepancies and obvious damage.
- Storing, stacking, or palletizing material in accordance with approved storage methods.
- Providing assistance regarding material requirements and completing all necessary documentation.

Accomplishments: Commended by supervisor for the quality and consistency of my performance.

Lincoln National Health Insurance   1990 - 1992
Pleasanton, California
Customer Service Support

EDUCATION

Completed Classes in General Education, Chabot Community College, Cupertino, California

STRENGTHS

Career reflects hard work, attention to detail, and the ability to meet exact specifications as well as cost, quality, safety and time objectives.

REFERENCES EXCELLENT AND AVAILABLE UPON REQUEST

JACK W. WRIGHT
2773 Carmen Avenue
Livermore, California 94550
Telephone: 510 443 4327

WELDER

Available to discuss a challenging and responsible position
where my education and experience can be fully
utilized to our mutual benefit.

Summary of Skills

......formal education....over 15 years experience in metal fabrication.....experienced in tool design......welding, MIG, TIG, and ARC......staff supervision and training...... purchasing...job costing....scheduling staff....inventory control....customer quotes.... quality control....reports....documentation....blueprints and sketches....maintenance of shop equipment......problem solving......ability to work under pressure......excellent communication skills....ability to work well with all levels of management and personnel....pride in quality performance and achievement....reliable....

PROFESSIONAL HIGHLIGHTS

Peterson Metal Fabrication   1992 to Present
Hayward, California
Weld Shop Supervisor
Position responsibilities include overseeing all weld shop operations; including the supervision and administration of 11 employees.
Accomplishments: Commended by supervisor for the quality and consistency of my performance.

Triple 8 Manufacturing Co.   1990 - 1992
San Leandro, California
Lead Welder
Responsible for supervision of three employees and overseeing all welding operations.
Accomplishments: Made significant contributions to the design of tooling for production in all areas.

Precision Metal Fabricators   1989 - 1990
Hayward, California
Shop Supervisor

EDUCATION

Completed Classes in General Education, Chabot Community College, Cupertino, California

STRENGTHS

Career reflects hard work, attention to detail, and the ability to meet exact specifications as well as cost, quality, safety and time objectives.

REFERENCES EXCELLENT AND AVAILABLE UPON REQUEST

RESUMÉ DATABASES

A resumé database is created when resumés are stored in a computer. Only the larger companies can afford the more expensive Optical Scanning Systems, but the larger companies only employ approximately 25% of the nation's work force. How can small business, employing 75% of the work force, compete?

There are a number of companies that specialize in creating resumé databases so companies of any size can find qualified job seekers for less than the cost of a classified ad. Many of these are specialized and cater to occupational groups or societies. For example, if you're getting out of the military you should check the Transition Bulletin Board (TBB). It's a sort of electronic help wanted column for separating servicemen.

One of the leaders of this new industry is SkillSearch - *and it's for everyone and does not require a computer or modem.* Carl Mullinax, the founder of SkillSearch says, "In addition to the rapidly growing optical scanning industry, which is principally used by Fortune 1000 companies to manage the large volume of unsolicited resumés that they receive, there are several national resumé databases that use new technology to warehouse huge amounts of information about individuals. These national databases simply match individuals in the database to the desired skill set from companies looking to fill open positions; a kind of electronic matchmaker.

It makes a great deal of sense for the company. Rather than use conventional methods of display advertising and professional recruiters (expensive and time consuming), companies can search these databases for the type of person they need to fill any position. The cost and time savings to the company is substantial. Obviously the individual who is either actively looking for, or simply interested in, learning about new career opportunities should ensure that their resumé is in one or more of these national databases. The cost of having your information entered on these databases is modest and you will be required to complete a member profile that is similar to a resumé, but organizes your skills in a standard format that facilitates searches.

SkillSearch utilizes advanced database systems to enter and track specific and very detailed information about each candidate's listing. SkillSearch can meet the needs of the most demanding company. Searches are performed using such criteria as geographic or relocation preference, salary requirements, experience, professional or technical skills, work history, SIC and SOC codes. SkillSearch will track and monitor information about virtually every aspect of the candidates career history and objectives. The service allows the member to update their resumé as necessary and members can request that their profile be permanently excluded from any search requested by their present (or other) employer, thus ensuring complete confidentiality.

SkillSearch has recognized a strong response outside large "blue chip" employers. Eight out of ten new jobs being created today are created by small companies with less than 100 employees. These small to medium sized employers are unlikely to invest in expensive optical scanning equipment and appreciate the affordability and flexibility of a national database such as SkillSearch."

I personally like the idea that a resumé is working for me (whether I'm employed or unemployed) 24 hours a day, 7 days a week. When I was doing the research for this book I looked into a number of resumé database companies, and found SkillSearch to be the best for most people. The fee of $65.00 buys a two year membership with unlimited updates (far longer than other memberships). Thereafter, members will be charged a modest $15.00 annual renewal fee. If you would like more information, or would like to enroll with SkillSearch, call toll free, 1-800-258-6641.

There are also online services, which require a computer and modem, and more of these services are popping up every day. CompuServe is one popular subscription service that has several items of interest for job seekers. One national magazine, "Online Access," lists Bulletin Board Services (BBS) for everything you can imagine, including phone numbers (local and long distance) to call for listings of government and private sector jobs.

PRINTING YOUR RESUMÉ

When you have finished the first draft of your resumé it should look a lot like the samples. Look it over and make sure there's a good balance between blank space and text. Paragraphs that are too long cause the reader to skip over them. Make sure that none of the letters, dashes, slashes, parentheses, or hyphens are too close.

Double check for typos and have someone help if possible. Typos do not belong on a resumé. Remember that *YOUR RESUMÉ MAKES A **FIRST IMPRESSION** BEFORE ANYONE SEES YOU.* When you're satisfied with everything, type the final copy (or have it typed, and remember that laser copies work best for optical scanning).

I recommend using the highest quality paper you can afford. Use light colors or white, but don't go to extremes like "hot pink" or other bright colors. Anything-but-white makes it easier to find your resumé among the other white papers on a desk.

The paper I recommend is made by Desktop Impressions, and is great for both optical scanners and people. They have a full line of resumé paper that is both stylish and practical, with silver or gold trim around the borders. To find the nearest retailer, or to order by phone, call toll-free 1-800-545-4628. It will make your resumé stand out from the competition and is well worth the extra effort.

If you're making copies at a print shop, don't run them on copiers that are used by the general public. These often have been dirtied by whiteout or damaged by paper clips. Have them run professionally by the personnel working there.

You should keep your originals in document protectors and save them in the event of a change in your phone number or address. It's also an excellent place to start the next time you need to write a resumé.

TIPS FOR YOUR JOB SEARCH

In most cases, I don't recommend that you go in person when you're looking for work. If you do, you will be asked to fill out an application when you submit your resumé. An application requests information that can be a <u>negative</u> - information such as salary desired and other things best discussed in an interview. For example, many people are willing to work for less money if it's with a good company with a fine career path and benefits. There's no place to explain this on an application, but it can be easily explained and appreciated in an interview. For this reason I recommend that you mail your resumé to prospective employers whenever possible.

Buy every major paper on Sunday for their Classified Ads. Every other job seeker will be doing this also, and they will all be mailing their resumés Monday morning with the idea of being the first. Don't be in such a hurry - wait until Wednesday or Thursday to mail yours. That way your resumé won't come in with all the rest and get lost in the shuffle. Trust me on this one; the company doesn't plan on filling the position on Monday. They plan on taking their time and looking the candidates over very carefully.

Go to every employment agency you can find. Most of the reputable ones don't charge the client and sometimes they find excellent jobs.

Go to a stationary or office supply store and purchase a paper-tablet-in-a-plastic-folder (I call them "interview folders"). Before you go to any interviews you need to do your homework so you're prepared to fill out the applications. Write down three personal and three professional references, along with their names, addresses and phone numbers. You will also need the addresses of companies you worked for, and the names and phone numbers of your supervisors. Write down any other information you might need for an application or interview. You should also bring an extra copy of your resumé and any letters or written commendations. You'll appear to be the kind of person who's not prepared if you have to say, "I'll phone you with that information later." **ALWAYS DO YOUR HOMEWORK!**

TIPS FOR THE INTERVIEW

Before I get into the interview, I would like to say something about the hiring process in a medium to large size company. Since companies have different policies, I will have to discuss this process in a general way, but it should give you an idea of what's involved.

Companies will usually call you to set up the time for the interview, and when you arrive the receptionist will ask you to fill out an application while you wait. Because you've done your "homework" as I previously suggested, the only problem you might have with the application is when it asks for your Salary Requirements. I suggest that you write "Open" or "Negotiable" in this space.

The next person you meet is usually someone from the personnel department. They will tell about the company history, the benefits, and how wonderful it is to work for them. If you don't know what the job pays, the most important part is when you are asked, "Do you have any questions?"

It's quite proper to say, "Yes, what is the salary range for this position?"

It's nice to have this information before being interviewed by the next person -- the Hiring Manager. Let's look at the manager's motives for a moment. The manager needs to hire someone who is the best qualified, and the less it costs the better. Hiring Managers need to get the job done and stay within their budget. They also want to hire someone they like (someone they can work with) and the resumé already tells what your skills are. The manager will usually want to know more about the level of your skills, so open up a little and show that you're likable. "Yes" and "No" answers don't reveal what kind of person you are.

There are three ways you can really do well in an interview -- **rehearse, rehearse, rehearse.** You can do this because there's one question that will always be asked, "Tell me a little about what you have done." The way I tell my clients to prepare for this is to first write down a one page answer. You won't like your first effort, so do it again and condense it to a half page. Then read it aloud several times and eliminate a few more words. You should now have it down to a paragraph that sounds smooth and organized when you read it aloud, and reading it aloud is <u>very important</u>. Have a friend ask this question and others from the "Sample Interview Questions" (next page). It's also a good idea to try to match skills that you've done in the past with the requirements of the position you're interviewing for.

SAMPLE INTERVIEW QUESTIONS

1. Why do you want this job?

2. What do you like the most about your present/last position?

3. Why do you want to leave your present/last job?

4. Tell me about your present/last position.

5. Tell me about a problem you had at work and how you solved it.

6. How long of a commitment could you make?

7. What type of environment do you like to work in?

8. Do you have any long term goals?

9. Why were you out of a job so long?

10. What are your strong points and weakness'?

11. How do you handle stress?

12. Why should I choose you for this position?

13. Tell me a little about yourself?

14. What are your salary requirements?

15. Do you have any questions?

Here's some sample questions to get you started.

1. When would you want me to start work?

2. Who will I be working for?

3. If this is a new position, where is the employee who had the job before me?

4. What would I be doing in a typical day?

5. What is the most important part of my duties?

6. Is this a full-time position?

Something new from the WinWay Corporation is a software program - "WinWay Job Interview for Windows." It teaches you how to interview with confidence... and win the job by practicing with over 200 most commonly asked questions. It provides hints and proven answers as you **hear** your male and female interviewers ask each question (with or without a sound card).

It shows the user how to prepare winning responses for questions about salary, benefits, skills and education, career goals, teamwork - even the more stressful and unlawful questions. You can save, evaluate, print your answers, and track your progress with colorful charts and graphs. To order, or get more information, call **1-800-4-WinWay.**

The interview is the most important part of your job search, and there is no time to think, only to perform. That's why it's so important to practice and rehearse the answer to for the interview. The difference in many cases in not <u>what</u> you say, but <u>how</u> you say it.

A question I often hear is, "I think my last boss might badmouth me if he/she is asked about a reference. What can I do?" The chances of a bad reference is slight in these days of employers giving only factual information such as dates of employment. If you worked for a small company or have any doubts, you can call and say that your lawyer wants to know what they will say about you. That will usually keep them in line.

Never say anything bad about any of your past employers, as it's easy to picture you badmouthing their company in the future. **No one likes chronic complainers**.

If the hiring manager has interviewed three candidates, and each has the same skills and experience, and the manager likes them all equally well, the candidate that asks for the least money will get the job.

When the job market is tight, I suggest you say something like the following when the manager asks you how much you need.

"I've always liked your company, and I'm willing to start near the low end until I've had a chance to prove myself, but I'd like to be reevaluated in six months." This will go a long way in helping you beat the competition, and can help the manager justify your selection. I speak from experience when I say that managers love it when you make their budget look good.

If you really want the job, be sure to get the manager's business card after the interview so you can write a "follow-up letter." The follow-up letter is one of the most overlooked employment tools. It should be personal (handwritten is acceptable), and should be a brief, polite letter thanking the manager for their time and courtesy (see the section on "Follow-Up Letters"). It should be written the same day as the interview when possible.

TIPS FOR YOUR CAREER

I can't take credit for the following tips as they've been around for ever, but I've found them to be good words to live by.

1. Always arrive at work before your boss.

2. Never bring your boss a problem without a solution. You're being paid to think, not to complain.

3. Help other people to network for jobs because what goes around comes around.

4. Don't use a sick day unless you're really sick.

5. Never count on anyone to keep a secret.

6. Treat everyone, from janitor to president with respect, and don't ever be patronizing.

7. Never take credit for someone else's work.

8. Avoid working on the weekends. Work longer during the week if you have to.

9. Always go to company parties and events... but don't drink to much!

10. Keep track of what you do and write it down; someone is sure to ask - usually your boss.

11. Always have an answer to the question "What would I do if I lost my job tomorrow?" And always have an up to date resumé ready.

12. There's no such thing as job security.

Well, that's about all I can think of to help in your job search - except that my phone number and address are on the sample resumés so you can call or write to me with your questions or comments. And hang onto this book for the next time you **"Hate-to-Write-a-Resumé!!!"**

Index

Index

SKILLSearch

☐ YES! Please enroll me in SKILLSearch today!

Name _____ Ref. TEP-115

Address _____

_____

Phone Number (_____) _____-_____

Method of Payment - $65.00 per person

☐   Check made out to SKILLSearch

☐   Mastercard   ☐ Visa   ☐   AMEX

Expiration Date: Month/Year _____/_____

Account Number: _____

Signature: _____

Return Address: **SKILLSearch Corporation**
3354 Perimeter Hill Drive, Suite 235
Nashville, TN 37211-4129

☐   YES! Please send me information about the many benefits of SKILLSearch Membership.

For faster service call 1-800-258-6641

TO ORDER BOOK(S), CALL LOGIN PUBLISHERS CONSORTIUM,
1-800-626-4330, OR FILL OUT THE COUPON BELOW AND MAIL TO:
Shastar Press, 2773 Carmen Avenue, Livermore, CA 94550 - Make check
or money order payable to Jack Wright.

Please send me _____ copies of "Resumés For People Who Hate to Write Resumés"
at $12.95 per copy. Shastar Press pays postage and handling.

Name _____

Address _____

City _____ State _____ Zip _____